'Fact and fiction interweave in Peter John Cooper's powerful study of the tensions that may have taken Thomas Hardy's first marriage close to breaking point. It was deservedly a huge success. Fine acting, superbly crafted dialogue, an excellent musical score from Roderick Skeaping and intelligent direction from Peter John Cooper himself make this a play to treasure.'

Jeremy Miles
Bournemouth Echo

'Four women weave fact with fiction and mix real people with characters from Hardy's novels in a fascinating insight into the troubled relationship between the author and his first wife Emma ... a tale that blends beautifully some of Hardy's own words into the largely fictional story and includes a neat sub-plot in which the original script of the writer's final novel, *Jude the Obscure*, teeters on the brink of extinction as it is tossed around between all four women ... a play that is almost certain to become a theatrical treasure in the future.'

Marion Cox
Dorset Echo

'This play is an exciting take on Hardy's women: the playwright has very cleverly interwoven the real and fictional women of Hardy's life and work.'

Mike Nixon
Secretary of the Thomas Hardy Society

She Opened the Door

The Wife and Women who Haunted Thomas Hardy

A play by
Peter John Cooper

Roving
Press

© 2012 Peter John Cooper

Published by Roving Press Ltd
4 Southover Cottages, Frampton, Dorset, DT2 9NQ, UK
Tel: +44 (0)1300 321531
www.rovingpress.co.uk

The rights of the author to be identified as the Author of this Work have been asserted in accordance with the Copyright, Designs and Patents Act 1988.

The play *She Opened the Door* is fully protected by copyright. All enquiries concerning performing rights, professional or amateur, should be directed to the author peterjohncooper@spyway.co.uk

First published 2012 by Roving Press Ltd

ISBN: 978-1-906651-183

British Library Cataloguing in Publication Data
A catalogue record for this book is available from the British Library

Cover design by Roving Press
Back cover photograph and frontispiece of Max Gate were taken with permission of the National Trust.

Set in 11.5/13 pt Minion by Beamreach (www.beamreachuk.co.uk)
Printed and bound by Henry Ling, at the Dorset Press, Dorchester, DT1 1HD

Contents

In memory of Norrie Woodhall 1905–2011,
the last surviving member of the Hardy Players, who knew Thomas
Hardy personally. She attended the Premiere of this play and
commented favourably upon it. She thereby completed a circle back to
Hardy himself.

*The Corn Exchange audience at the Premiere included the Mayor of Dorchester
Leslie Phillips, the Mayoress and, between them, Norrie Woodhall.*

Acknowledgements

Thanks to Jane McKell of AsOne Theatre Company for the original commission and without whose encouragement and stern deadlines this play would never have been written. A play for theatre is inevitably part of a collaborative process, with many people involved, so I must acknowledge the contributions of the actors, stage crew and other professionals, whose names are mentioned elsewhere. But, of course, a play cannot exist without an audience so I am delighted to acknowledge the contribution made by the hundreds of folk who came and added that essential ingredient. Mike Nixon, Secretary of the Thomas Hardy Society, has been supportive and helpful all the way through the project.

The photographs within the text of the play, Introduction and Premiere Production are by Ian Brooke of Brooke Studios, Weymouth. That of the performers in Max Gate garden is by Iain McKell. The author's photograph is by Danika Westwood. Photographs of Emma Hardy, Florence Henniker, Jemima Hardy and the Hardy Players are courtesy of the Dorset History Centre. The cartoon 'Is this the way to Wareham, please?' is reproduced with permission of *Punch* Ltd (www.punch. co.uk).

I also thank Elinor Cooper for reading the text and Holly Cooper and Clare Shervin for their endless support.

She Opened the Door

She opened the door of the West to me,
With its loud sea-lashings,
And cliff-side clashings
Of waters rife with revelry.
She opened the door of Romance to me,
The door from a cell
I had known too well,
Too long, till then, and was fain to flee.
She opened the door of a Love to me,
That passed the wry
World-welters by
As far as the arching blue the lea.
She opens the door of the Past to me,
Its magic lights,
Its heavenly heights,
When forward little is to see!

Thomas Hardy, 1913

Introduction

It is 2007. I am sitting at a table in the bar of a leisure centre in North Dorset. The place is cheery in a strictly contemporary sort of way. Pale wood laminates, chrome fittings, halogen ceiling lights. Behind me at the bar four men are lounging. They are discussing sheep prices or something mundane. They go on to argue about last night's television. They gossip about what has happened to one of their mates on holiday. I am suddenly shocked into awareness. It dawns on me that I am listening to four voices straight out of a novel by Thomas Hardy. By keeping my eyes closed I can imagine myself in the parlour of the Pure Drop Inn. These men, for all they are wearing 21st-century leisure wear rather than smock frocks, are characters exactly as Hardy would have recognised them. Apart from the references to *Strictly Come Dancing*, if I wrote down what they said I could insert it into any of the novels and it would not stand out as being in any way extraordinary.

The point that came to me was that Hardy was not only a great and accurate recorder of the rural scene but also a contemporary writer writing about contemporary issues, and when we consign him to the rural backwater of Wessex in our imaginations we are missing something vital and immediate. What those issues were have become clearer to me over the years. Not through any great attempt at scholarship; there are swathes of Hardy landscape where I have never trodden and where I have been it is only by following the paths of the biographers and academics. No, anything I have understood is through my attempts at interpreting his works for the stage.

Some years ago I was commissioned to write a couple of adaptations of Thomas Hardy novels for the theatre. Whilst working on these I was struck by the pivotal role that women play in the dramas. In *The Mayor of Casterbridge*, for instance, it is Susan Henchard's decision to go with the sailor that sets the whole drama in motion. And her decision to return that fans the flames of the tragedy. I also noticed how many strong women surrounded Hardy in his own life, all of whom could have been said to have Opened the Door to his talent (I'm sure you know where that line comes from). And in later years his attitude to women has been the source for considerable debate, much of which I disagree

1

Some street publicity for the play She Opened the Door *outside Michael Henchard's house, South Street, Dorchester.*

with strenuously. So when Jane McKell invited me to write a play about Hardy's women I had the theme and subject matter ready to go. I also realised there was a whole story to be investigated about how *Jude the Obscure* became his last complete novel. Something happened around 1895, the time that *Jude* was published in novel form, that affected his desire to write novels and changed his relationship with his wife Emma dramatically. This was one of those great turning points in a life that we dramatists seek out. We snuffle about in our imaginations asking how this or that might have come about and what the outcome may be.

She Opened the Door is a fantasy. The events are fabricated but I have tried to slip my story into the little chinks and crevices between recorded facts. There is no record that Hardy's mother and Florence Henniker visited Max Gate on the day in question but it's not beyond the realms of possibility that they could have done so. At the same time, the characters represent more than just the real-life personalities of historical record. In order to show something of Hardy's relationship with his family I have conflated some of the recorded views of his actual mother with those of his grandmother and sisters. Similarly 'The Other Woman' is based

2

around the character of Florence Henniker but also includes material from some of his other adoring admirers and helpers.

To develop the fantasy still further I have drawn on Hardy's own writings and put them straight or twisted into the mouths of my characters. Hardy himself always claimed that he only based one character of his novels completely on a real person. But those of us who write for a living know how profoundly unlikely that assertion must be. I have supposed that many of the words that occur in his writing he will have overheard from his family and friends and used either consciously or unconsciously.

It might amuse you to try to see where I have fitted some of Hardy's own words and situations into the dialogue. I have drawn from at least five of the novels and several of the short stories and poems. But don't ask me to help you out because they have become so deeply embedded that, at this stage, I genuinely can't identify them all myself.

***

The whole process of writing and producing this play has reverberated with echoes of Hardy the man. At the beginning I made a number of visits to Max Gate, where the National Trust is trying to reinstate some of the original character, and idled about the garden looking for inspiration. Here I worked out exactly where the events would have taken place and where characters would arrive from and disappear to. I imagined the maid wandering the garden looking for the precious package she had been entrusted with. I pictured Emma storming out of the side door on her way to consign the package to the bonfire. I could see where Mrs Henniker would arrive on her bicycle up the drive and I visualised the bench where Hardy's mother would take up her position and listen in to private conversations and from where she would cause her mischief. And there was the gate in the wall where Hardy himself would (and did in real life) disappear to be out of the way of trouble. It was all there before me and I didn't have to invent a single piece of the setting.

And then there was Hardy the writer haunting the process. After the initial research and writing during the winter of 2009, the public read-through was held in the glorious Victorian Gallery of the County Museum in Dorchester in March 2010. The museum contains a huge Hardy collection and archive. Here is the actual study in which he wrote, transported in its entirety from Max Gate, as well as a collection

In the Victorian Gallery of the Dorset County Museum, a packed audience for the read-through.

of his manuscripts and letters. The audience at the museum event was well aware of the connections and the piece was received warmly and enthusiastically.

Even Hardy's characters could not be avoided. To promote the production, parts of scenes were performed in the street outside the house that is the supposed residence of Michael Henchard in South Street, Dorchester.

The premiere performance was held at the Corn Exchange as the final event of the 19th International Hardy Society Conference on 1 August 2010. Here walked the ghosts of Bathsheba Everdene and Michael Henchard. And here was Henchard's real-life counterpart – the current Mayor of Casterbridge. As an embellishment there was the attendance by Norrie Woodhall, who at the time was 105 and the last remaining person alive to know Hardy, as a member of the Hardy Players, the company that Hardy assembled to perform adaptations of his own novels.

But for me, the most moving performance was that during the afternoon of September 2011 when we were invited by the National Trust to perform in the garden of Max Gate on the exact spot where I had set the action. We chose the acting area so that the actors would be lit by the afternoon sun and entrances could be made from the side door of the house and from the shadows of the trees and hedges. A hundred supporters packed into the small side garden and the actors pushed themselves to the limit to be heard. The sun shone, spectators lounged on the grass, cream teas were consumed, making it an altogether magical afternoon. Most of the audience could see the room where Hardy's study was situated over the shoulders of the actors. There was a real feeling that Hardy himself could be working in his room or pottering about in the vegetable garden through the hedge. Somebody produced a photograph showing the Hardy Players performing *Tess* in exactly the same spot we had chosen. Everyone knew it was a very special day and emotions were running high.

The whole process, and the continuing proximity of Hardy's shade, gave me an altogether deeper understanding of the writer and his life. I have made some notes about what I learnt from writing *She Opened the Door*. You will find them in an Afterword at the end of the script itself.

In the garden at Max Gate.

She Opened the Door

Premiere Production

First performed by AsOne Theatre Company at the Corn Exchange, Dorchester on 1 August 2010 for the 19th International Thomas Hardy Conference and Festival. It had the following cast:

The Wife	Jane McKell
The Mother	Mary Lou Delaplanque
The Other Woman	Tricia Lewis
The Maid	Dani Bright

(The part of The Mother was played later in the tour by Julia Savill.)

Directed by	Peter John Cooper
Music specially composed by	Roderick Skeaping
Designed by	Annette Sumption
Costumes made by	Emily Smith (Amazing Emily's)
Audio visual by	Kevin Butcher
Lighting by	John Newton
Stage management by	Brendon Gregg
	Ian Rixon
	Sarah Warren

AsOne Theatre Company was founded by its current Artistic Director, Jane McKell, and has been touring Dorset and the South West of England since 2004. It became a not-for-profit organisation in 2006 with aims to support employment for, and collaboration with, professional arts practitioners in Dorset, and to specialise in commissioning and touring original, thought-provoking theatre with a focus on local history, culture and heritage created with a powerful mix of drama, music and projected image. A further aim is to give a voice to Dorset communities, telling their unique stories, using arts professionals to engage with the wider community including schools, youth groups and museums as well as theatres. *A String of Pearls*, a musical play, was devised from some 200 letters sent to the company from women and children with memories of

The Premiere at the Corn Exchange, Dorchester, showing the cast and crew with the Mayor of Dorchester Leslie Phillips and (centre) Norrie Woodhall.

World War II and toured in association with the Royal British Legion. AsOne has made strong links with businesses who invest in projects in return for heightened branding, staff and client rewards and workshops. This engagement resulted in the theatre company being awarded the SW Arts and Business Heightened Branding Award 2007 with their partner Curves Ladies Fitness and health franchisees across Wessex. In 2009 AsOne was selected to be one of three finalists out of 50 nominees for the Dorset Business Awards Most Creative Project of the Year Award for its play about five Portland couples' journey into parenthood, *Hey Baby!* (in association with Action for Children and Curves) and *Hey Baby-Baby*, a teenage pregnancy prevention project.

Dramatis Personae and Setting

The Wife	Emma, Thomas Hardy's first wife. She is 55 years old. A lover of animals and known locally for her eccentricities.
The Mother	Jemima, Thomas Hardy's mother. She is 82 years old and thoroughly disliked by her daughter-in-law. The sentiment is mutual.
The Other Woman	Based on Florence Henniker (the Honourable Mrs Arthur Henniker), a novelist and advocate of women's rights. She is 40 years old, a vigorous and beautiful woman.
The Maid	Amelia, a young woman from Dorchester, who has been ruined in Bournemouth and has returned with a baby. She is 19 years old.

The setting is Emma's private garden next to Max Gate, the house that Thomas Hardy has designed and built at the side of the turnpike leading out of Dorchester.

Two garden benches are right and left and a smouldering fire basket is upstage just off centre. An entrance right leads to the side door of the house and left to the rest of the garden. Another entrance through the audience leads to the drive and the front gate.

It is an afternoon in September 1895.

ACT 1

We are in the garden of Thomas Hardy's house at Max Gate. Smoke drifts across the stage. Through it we see the figure of Thomas's wife Emma tearing pages from a notebook and consigning them to a large, smouldering bonfire. She is agitated and seems in a barely contained frenzy. Now she has a large brown-paper parcel tied with string. It may be the manuscript of a novel. In her excitable state she seems about to cast the package into the flames.

EMMA

Go to the Devil, Thomas Hardy. And your filthy book, and let you burn in Hell with the pages. Devil take Sue and Arabella and most of all Jude the Obscene. Go to Hell, the lot of you.

[Music. Voices of THE MOTHER, THE OTHER WOMAN and THE MAID can be heard through the smoke from various points in the garden]

'Go to Hell, the lot of you.'

THE MOTHER

I opened the door.

THE OTHER WOMAN

I opened the door.

THE MAID

I opened the door.

THE MOTHER

You? Mrs Hardy?

THE OTHER WOMAN

You? Mrs Hardy?

THE MAID

Mrs Hardy? I opened the door ...
Mrs Hardy ... Mrs Hardy.

EMMA

I'm burning it. Getting rid of the obscenity once and for all.

THE MAID

I opened the door and it was gone.

EMMA

I know who you are. Sue Bridehead, Mrs Yeobright, Tess Durberville, Mrs William Marchmill. I know you all. I know because I let you all in. I let you inhabit this world. I helped build the places where you live. Thomas would never, not on his own. Would never. He needed me to help make you. I did the work. I copied it all. Long into the night. My eyes burning with the strain. And I gave him the ideas. And he repays me like this. Oh, I knew it would come to no good. I should have been there. It was me. I opened the door. I opened the door to his genius. We lived like gypsies. We lived in poverty. Because I believed in him. I believed in the work. I gave up everything to be with him when he needed me.

[The women's voices fade into the smoke]

THE MOTHER

You opened the door?

THE OTHER WOMAN

You opened the door?

THE MAID

You opened the door?

THE MOTHER

You? Mrs Hardy?

THE OTHER WOMAN

You? Mrs Hardy?

THE MAID

Mrs Hardy? I opened the door ...

[Music fades]

EMMA

Go to Hell, the lot of you.

THE MAID

Mrs Hardy ... Mrs Hardy.

EMMA

I'm burning it. Getting rid of the obscenity once and for all.

THE MAID

I opened the door and it was gone.

EMMA

How could he?

THE MAID

That's Mr Hardy's book you've got there. Mr Hardy asked me to take it down to the post office. When I've finished here. He left it on the hall table. But when I opened the door to come out it was gone.

EMMA

It's a fantasy. A tissue of lies. It's all lies.

THE MAID

It's the truth. On the Bible ...

EMMA

The book, girl. It's a tissue of lies.

THE MAID

Isn't that what all books are, Mrs Hardy? Pardon me for speaking out. I think you ought to be careful, Mrs Hardy. If that gets burnt I'll get into terrible trouble.

EMMA

This is my life.

THE MAID

Your life? It's my job.

EMMA

No, I don't mean that. Well yes, in a manner of speaking. No. You're twisting things.

It's my life. Mine and that woman. That other woman. Those other women.

[She suddenly realises THE MAID is wearing an extraordinary old-fashioned costume with large hat]

THE MAID

Shall I fetch Mr Hardy, Madam?

EMMA

Good heavens, girl. What are you wearing? Go and take that off at once and put on your proper dress. The one I bought you for six shillings. Mr Hardy is expecting visitors today.

THE MAID

Yes. I was going to say ... It was Mr Hardy's idea. The girl who was going to play Tess has got a cold. And I've read it so many times I know it off by heart. Mr Hardy said ... After I've taken the package to the post.

EMMA

He's just about to destroy both our lives. Once and for all.

THE MAID

Who, Madam?

EMMA

He wrote about us, about our marriage, secret things. Things that are only proper between man and wife.

THE MAID

Yes, Madam. If you say so, Madam. I only read books that you choose now. And you never choose those. Do you? Oh yes. I came to say ...

EMMA

This is madness. Mad, mad, mad.

THE MAID

... To say ... that there are callers, Madam.

EMMA

Callers? What sort of callers?

THE MAID

Two ladies, Madam.

                         EMMA
Ladies?

                        THE MAID
Mr Hardy's mother and his sister Mary, Madam.

                         EMMA
Ladies? They are not Ladies.

                        THE MAID
No, Madam?

                         EMMA
They are women. They are village women.

                        THE MAID
Yes, Madam. If you say so, Madam.

                         EMMA
How old are you, girl?

                        THE MAID
Nineteen and a half, Madam.

                         EMMA
And yet, at your age ... Everything that's happened ... You still do not
know the difference between women and Ladies?

                        THE MAID
No, Madam. I mean yes, Madam.

                         EMMA
If anyone's mad ... What are you doing standing there gawping, girl?

                        THE MAID
I wondered what I should say to them.

To whom?

THE MAID
The Ladies ... The women, Madam. What should I say to them?

EMMA
Goodness only knows. Whatever it is that people like you and they talk
about over the garden fence. Village gossip, I suppose. Who is expecting
a baby, who has had a baby, who was not in church on Sunday. How
should I know?

THE MAID
Should I ask them to wait? Until you've finished ... whatever it is you are
doing?

EMMA
You may tell them to wait until Hell freezes over.

THE MAID
Perhaps I'd better tell Mr Hardy, then.

EMMA
Of course. It is his party. They've come to see the great author. Not his
wife. Where is Mr Hardy?

THE MAID
I can't find him. That's why I came to you. He was talking to the men.
Putting up the tent. He seems to have wandered off. He asked me to
take that package to the post office.

EMMA
Very well. You may tell them ... those women ... that we are not at home.
Mr Hardy is too busy making arrangements.

THE MAID
Very good, Madam. And the others?

EMMA

What others?

THE MAID

Women. Men and women and Ladies and Gentlemen. Mr Hardy's entertainment. People from the town.

EMMA

They are no concern of mine. They have come to see Mr Hardy. Not me.

THE MAID

And shall I take the package, now?

EMMA

No. I have not decided. What I shall do with it. Yet. But I shall see that I put a stop to it at all costs.

[EMMA exits, leaving THE MAID undecided what to do]

THE MAID

Mr Hardy said .... Mrs Hardy! [*shouts*]. You baint nothing but a stupid stuck-up cow, Mrs Hardy. With your fah lah ways.

[THE MOTHER enters from the drive where she has been waiting]

THE MOTHER

I hope you're not talking about me, my dear.

THE MAID

Oh, not you. The other one. Begging your pardon. I was talking to the other Mrs Hardy.

THE MOTHER

So it seems. And what did she say? About me?

THE MAID

She said you were to wait. I suppose.

THE MOTHER

I'll wait here, then.

[She makes herself comfortable on one of the benches]

THE MAID

This is Mrs Hardy's garden. She may not ... Yes ... I'll go and fetch Mr Hardy then. And then I've got to get to the post. If I can get that parcel back.

THE MOTHER

'Tis a fine house they have here.

THE MAID

Yes, indeed.

THE MOTHER

Built it himself. You know that. Well, he drew it up and his brother did the building. 'Tis not Solomon's Temple but 'twill do. Mr Hardy learnt to be an architect, you know.

THE MAID

Yes. It's very ... modern.

THE MOTHER

It's very sound built. You don't like it?

THE MAID

I don't think Missus likes it.

THE MOTHER

Oh?

THE MAID

'Taint big enough for her. Nor grand enough, neither. And too near the turnpike.

17

THE MOTHER

How do you find her? The other Mrs Hardy? Do you find her difficult?

THE MAID

No ... No. She took me in. Not many others would've. There's others round here would've sent me begging from door to door. No, she means well. She's just ... She gets me to read to her. I read well. I passed sixth standard at the National School under a London mistress. Afore I went up over to Bournemouth and ... She likes me to read. Yes, I go and read, Mrs Hardy; but as to getting my lady to hearken, that's more than a team of six horses could force her to do.

THE MOTHER

'Tis the same story, then?

THE MAID

Yes. Eaten out with listlessness. She's neither sick nor sorry, but how dull and dreary she is, only herself can tell. When I get there in the morning, there she is sitting up in bed, for my lady don't care to get up; and then she makes me bring this book and that book, till the bed is heaped up with immense volumes that half bury her, making her look, as she leans upon her elbow, like the stoning of Stephen. She yawns; then she looks towards the tall glass; then she looks out at the weather, mooning her great black eyes, and fixing them on the sky as if they stuck there, while my tongue goes flick-flack along, a hundred and fifty words a minute; then she looks at the clock; then she asks me what I've been reading.

THE MOTHER

Ah, poor soul! No doubt she says in the morning, 'Would God it were evening,' and in the evening, 'Would God it were morning,' like the disobedient woman in Deuteronomy.

Do you know this is the only time I've ever been here?

THE MAID

No. No, I don't know. Me only being here a little while myself.

18

THE MOTHER

Ah, poor woman! The state she finds herself in … she've took against
me as well.

THE MAID

But you're … Mr Hardy's mother. She can't …

THE MOTHER

She can and she have.

THE MAID

This place … Promise you won't tell.

'Promise you won't tell.'

[She sits next to THE MOTHER on the bench]

The other Mrs Hardy … It's as cold as the tomb. She invites the children
in. To run in the garden. She likes to see them, she says. Running this
way and that among the flowers. She shows them all the little creatures

crawling in the grass and the birds in the trees. She loves the birds and animals as if they were ... If it wasn't for them it would just be a graveyard. I best go and find Mr Hardy then.

[Exit]

THE MOTHER
Yes, 'tis all a mother can bear sometimes. I tried to warn him.

She shouldn't have come here, I suppose. 'Tis not to her taste one bit. No. Not one bit. Filling up the garden with other people's childer when she have none of her own. Young Tommy should've gone to London and taken her too. There's no glory in being a writer down here. He should have stuck to London where he's suited and left Dorset for the likes of we.

[The music of piano and fiddles as the parlour dance begins]

> *Fifty years have passed me by*
> *And changed the face of all in turns.*
> *The gardens, orchards, fields of corn*
> *Were slopes of bramble, furze and thorn.*
> *The road a narrow path with ferns*
> *Obscured the passers-by.*
>
> *Her garden here so out of place*
> *Where once the turnpike keeper slept*
> *And let the rumbling traffic pass.*
> *His dogs stood yapping on the grass*
> *While lowing herds and horses kept*
> *Their steady onward pace.*
>
> *People, like the scurrying ants,*
> *Passed to and fro and to and fro:*
> *Processions since the distant past.*
> *The progress of the years so fast*
> *That dead men sleeping there below*
> *Have never made to stop their dance.*

'Fifty years have passed me by.'

[The music continues. THE MOTHER is transported back to her youth and she dances an arthritic quadrille with an imaginary partner. During this THE OTHER WOMAN enters from the gate pushing a bicycle. THE OTHER WOMAN is wearing a bicycling suit with tweed knickerbockers. She props her bicycle against the other bench and joins the dance. The music stops]

No 'tis not for the likes of her. Cold as a tomb, right enough.

[She suddenly realises that she has been dancing with a real partner]

I'm sorry, Sir. I got carried away.

THE OTHER WOMAN
You must be the estimable Mrs Hardy.

THE MOTHER
I am only Mr Hardy's mother. There is another Mrs Hardy.

THE OTHER WOMAN
Yes, yes. I know her. And never say 'Only a mother'. It is a great calling.

THE MOTHER
[Peering myopically at THE OTHER WOMAN]

Wait on, you baint a he. You be a she. I'm getting on and my eyesight baint what it used to be.

THE OTHER WOMAN
A common enough mistake. I'm in my bicycling dress. It is the coming thing, bicycling. Health-giving and invigorating. And it enables many women to get out and about in a way they couldn't have dreamed of a few years ago.

THE MOTHER
I don't know overmuch about coming things. I used to; but then they came and they went. And then I didn't know them anymore. I'm afraid I'm a simple country soul.

THE OTHER WOMAN
Not so simple. Thomas ... Mr Hardy speaks highly of you.

THE MOTHER
He does?

THE OTHER WOMAN
You've read widely. He always says you gave him his love of literature. You sent him to school. You encouraged him to go to London. A lesson to all mothers. You thought only of him.

THE MOTHER
He was a sickly child. When he was born, the midwife didn't think he'd any breath, but then she sees a little movement and then he plims up all pink and new. But I knew he was never going to work for his living like his father and uncles.

THE OTHER WOMAN
But Mr Hardy's father. Was he interested in literature?

THE MOTHER

He was a good man, Tommy's father, but he was not a pusher. We could've moved closer to Dorchester. Closer to where there might have been some business. But he preferred lying in the sun on a bank of thyme or camomile with the grasshoppers leaping over him and going for his solitary walks on the heath with his telescope. And then Tommy came to me and said he never wanted to grow up, it broke my heart. I knew he could make something of himself.

THE OTHER WOMAN

So, it was all owing to you? Thomas's literary abilities?

THE MOTHER

He was a solitary child. Didn't play with the others much. He was weak. We thought he wasn't living when he was born. I had to look after him all through childhood. But he was bright as a button. He could read as soon as he could walk. We had good times together. But he was a sensitive child. When his father played the fiddle he could be moved to tears. I even got him an old table piano he could pick out tunes on. He should have been parson. But I persuaded him against that.

THE OTHER WOMAN

And you read to him. *Paradise Lost*. It was his favourite work of literature.

THE MOTHER

And now I can't read a thing and nobody listens to what I have to say. 'Tis as Job said, 'Now they that are younger than I have me in derision, whose fathers I would have disdained to have set with the dogs of my flock.'

You know a deal about him. Be you close?

THE OTHER WOMAN

Goodness me. He has confided in me. From time to time. I am a novelist myself. We have written a book together. Some little success. I have been able to help him. From time to time. I am afraid there is no-one to introduce us properly. My name is Henniker. Thomas ... Mr Hardy may have mentioned me.

23

THE MOTHER

Oh, yes. The Honourable Mrs Arthur Henniker. He talks to me when he can. When he can get away from this place.

THE OTHER WOMAN

And you have read all his books?

THE MOTHER

No. I've never read a line of them.

THE OTHER WOMAN

You disapprove? Not suitable for your eyes?

THE MOTHER

Why no. But I have had them read to me.

THE OTHER WOMAN

Ah, no. I forgot. Your eyesight. And do you like them?

THE MOTHER

Too many 'Thick'ns' and 'zoos I did' for my taste. He shouldn't have made such fun of us country folk. But folk in the town liked 'em well enough, I believe. He should have kept to writing about London. What happens there is more important. And left us folk be.

The boy was crazy for books, that he was. It runs in our family rather. 'Tom, my child, don't you ever marry', I said. ''Tisn't for the Hardys to take that step any more. I told 'n to get himself off to London. That's where you can be somebody.

'It is a city of light,' I said. 'The tree of knowledge grows there. It is a place that teachers of men spring from and go to. It is what you may call a castle, manned by scholarship and learning.'

And do you know what he said?

'It would just suit me.' But he wambled around. Got married and then came back just the same. Why would he do that?

24

THE OTHER WOMAN
And do you still disapprove?

THE MOTHER
Of what?

THE OTHER WOMAN
Of marriage.

THE MOTHER
You be a married woman?

THE OTHER WOMAN
I have a very good husband. Arthur. He is solid, reliable. He enables me to keep a good house. My children are well cared for. He gives me freedom to come and go.

'You be a married woman?'

25

THE MOTHER

On your – bicycle.

THE OTHER WOMAN

As I said, it is the symbol of freedom that will enable many women to break free of their chains.

THE MOTHER

So you thought you'd bicycle to Dorset?

THE OTHER WOMAN

Well, from the station.

THE MOTHER

To see an old friend?

THE OTHER WOMAN

Yes ... Emma Hardy.

THE MOTHER

And now I feel so drowsy. 'Tis a fair way from Bockhampton when you haven't got a bicycle. I would've done it easy enough once. And I had Mary to lean on today. You won't mind if I just sit down here ... would you?

THE OTHER WOMAN

You are so hot.

[She takes a small bottle from the basket on the bicycle]

Here, let me put some cologne on your brow.

[THE MOTHER collapses onto the bench. THE OTHER WOMAN cradles her, dabbing her brow. EMMA enters carrying the parcel]

EMMA

Good lord! What are you doing, man? This is my garden. It is a respectable place. I'll have none of that here.

[THE OTHER WOMAN turns to confront EMMA]

Heavens! Mrs Henniker!

[EMMA is thrown into confusion. She attempts a small curtsy and drops the package she is still carrying]

Mrs Henniker. I thought ... Your dress. Are you to be in the drama?

[THE OTHER WOMAN laughs out loud and picks up the package and places it on the bench next to THE MOTHER]

THE OTHER WOMAN
Emma, my dear. I came here by bicycle.

EMMA
Yes, so I see. Your dress is entirely ... appropriate.

THE OTHER WOMAN
So, Thomas is holding a garden party. I seem to have arrived at a good time.

EMMA
Yes, some people from the town. They are enacting a small part of Mr Hardy's work. As a drama. And I see some of them have wandered in here ... Excuse me. I'll get rid of the interlopers and then we may have a pleasant conversation. A cup of tea inside where it is more salubrious.

[EMMA nudges THE MOTHER to get her to wake up. EMMA tries to rescue the parcel but THE MOTHER turns over and leans heavily on it]

You should be going. You oughtn't to be here. Mr Hardy is at the other end of the garden.

THE OTHER WOMAN
Emma dear. Thomas's mother is feeling faint from the heat.

THE MOTHER
'Tis a very fine garden you have here.

EMMA

I like to think so.

THE MOTHER

Do you have a garden, Milady, Mrs er ...?

THE OTHER WOMAN

Yes, I do.

THE MOTHER

Very fine roses. Very modern.

EMMA

Yes, they last longer.

THE MOTHER

These modern ones, I don't like them so much. Not so much scent as the old-fashioned ones.

EMMA

No, no. But they do last.

THE MOTHER

Ah yes ... they do last. Very fine considering.

EMMA

Considering what?

THE MOTHER

Considering the soil. Very thin up here. Not much cover. Mind you, I expect there's plenty dug in makes them grow.

EMMA

Dug in?

THE MOTHER

Dead matter.

EMMA

Compost, you mean?

THE MOTHER

Blood and bone. Blood and bone.

EMMA

I use an onion.

THE MOTHER

An onion?

EMMA

Dug into the roots. It makes the flowers smell more sweetly.

THE MOTHER

Do you know about such things, Milady?

THE OTHER WOMAN

Please, just call me Mrs Henniker. You are with a friend.

THE MOTHER

Ah, old habits die hard. I was in service once. I saw a bit of the world and I might've gone to London but it wasn't to be. I forbade my daughters, Kate and Mary, from doing the same. I paid for them to go to college and now Mary's the headmistress of a girls' school.

THE OTHER WOMAN

Bravo. We should enable all girls to have the freedom to choose a better life.

THE MOTHER

Turn over thic flat stone. See they slugs? Hiding away from the heat of the day. Taking them all in all branches – which do you think are the most hardy? The black ones or the brown ones? Which ones are tough and which ones tender? Why do you think there are so many at this time of year? And what do you think is the better way of exterminating them? The boot heel or the scissors?

EMMA
I am a friend of all God's creatures. They will all run alive in my part of
the garden.

THE MOTHER
So they crawl up your roses, between the thorns, artful as they are, and
gobble up your beautiful, late, modern flowers.

EMMA
Amelia! Come here, girl. Now. This ... person is to wait elsewhere.
Where Mr Hardy can find her.

[THE MAID enters]

Good grief, girl. You've still got that ridiculous costume on. Take that
off at once.

[EMMA hisses in THE MAID's ear]

Do you know who this is? It's the Honourable Mrs Arthur Henniker,
daughter of Lord Houghton and Lady Crewe.

THE MAID
[To THE OTHER WOMAN]

Beg your pardon, Madam. It's Mr Hardy. He wants me to take part in
his entertainment. I'm to be Tess of the D'Urbervilles. The other girl
didn't show up.

EMMA
That is most inappropriate.

THE OTHER WOMAN
Theatricals! How jolly. Do you think he has any other parts going?

THE MAID
There's a big hamper of costumes in his study.

EMMA

We have so much to discuss ...

THE OTHER WOMAN

Will we have to learn lines? I know many passages by heart.

THE MAID

I think we're only meant to be doing small parts from all his books.
And reading them mostly.

EMMA

I've never heard anything so ridiculous. It is so demeaning. A
housemaid playing Tess.

THE MAID

But I do know them pat. I've read them over and over. Especially Tess.

[Acting]

*'Tis quite true. If I had gone for love o' you, if I had ever sincerely loved
you, if I loved you still, I should not so loathe and hate myself for my
weakness as I do now! ... My eyes were dazed by you for a little, and that
was all.*

Then he shrugs his shoulders.

I didn't understand your meaning till it was too late.

THE OTHER WOMAN

That's what every woman says.

THE MAID

*How can you dare to use such words! My God! I could knock you out of
the gig! Did it never strike your mind that what every woman says some
women may feel?'*

*[THE MAID suddenly makes a charge for THE OTHER WOMAN,
fists flying]*

31

'I could knock you out of the gig!'

EMMA
[Horrified at this breach of etiquette]

Amelia. Stop it. Stop it at once. Our guest.

THE OTHER WOMAN
She is playing the part. Word perfect, too. If I remember correctly. And I am speaking the words of the dastardly Alec D'Urberville

Very well, I am sorry to wound you. I did wrong – I admit it. Only you needn't be so everlastingly flinging it in my face. I am ready to pay to the uttermost farthing. You know you need not work in the fields or the dairies again. You know you may clothe yourself with the best, instead of in the bald plain way you have lately affected, as if you couldn't get a ribbon more than you earn.

THE MAID
I have said I will not take anything more from you, and I will not – I cannot! I should be your creature to go on doing that, and I won't!

32

THE OTHER WOMAN

One would think you were a princess from your manner, in addition to a true and original D'Urberville – ha! ha! Well, Tess, dear, I can say no more. I suppose I am a bad fellow – a damn bad fellow. I was born bad, and I have lived bad, and I shall die bad in all probability. But, upon my lost soul, I won't be bad towards you again, Tess. And if certain circumstances should arise – you understand – in which you are in the least need, the least difficulty, send me one line, and you shall have by return whatever you require.

THE MAID

And then there's kissing and such like.

THE OTHER WOMAN
[Continues]

Well, you are absurdly melancholy, Tess. I have no reason for flattering you now, and I can say plainly that you need not be so sad. You can hold your own for beauty against any woman of these parts, gentle or simple; I say it to you as a practical man and well-wisher. If you are wise you will show it to the world more than you do before it fades …

EMMA

Amelia. I thought I said this … person was to wait elsewhere. Escort her to Mr Hardy's part of the garden.

[EMMA nudges THE MOTHER in the ribs in an attempt to get at the parcel while trying to retain her dignity]

THE OTHER WOMAN

What are you doing? Are you not aware that this is Mr Hardy's own mother?

EMMA

Yes, but we don't want to be bothered with her doings, do we? We have other things to discuss. I wish to raise funds for the anti-vivisection society and I am thinking of holding a garden party of my own. What do you think?

THE OTHER WOMAN
I think it will be late in the year. There will be fog and dew on the grass.

EMMA
Next year, then. Next summer. Amelia!

[There is a brief tussle over the sleeping MOTHER. EMMA tries to grab the parcel unsuccessfully. THE OTHER WOMAN looks on puzzled]

THE OTHER WOMAN
Do you not realise that this good woman is the fountainhead of all Mr Hardy's genius?

EMMA
I'm sure God above was responsible for that. And others of us here on earth who recognised it and nurtured it. He always wanted to go to university. Perhaps it would have been better if he had been able. It might have shown him a better, more religious way.

THE MAID
[Now has the parcel in her hand]

I'd best fetch Mr Hardy.

[THE MAID goes to exit holding the parcel triumphantly. But by some sleight of hand, THE OTHER WOMAN takes it from her]

Mr Hardy. Mr Hardy ...

[Exit]

EMMA
You still have not told me why you came today.

THE OTHER WOMAN
Trying out the new machine. A small holiday in Dorset. I came by train and then *á la veloze* up the hill. Such fun.

[Sings]

Through the clouds of dust I come
On my bicycle. On my bicycle
Racing forward, racing forward
Into the future, into the future
Putting the past behind me.

So I am found on Ingpen Beacon,
or on Wylls-Neck to the west,
Or else on homely Bulbarrow,
or little Pilsdon Crest,

Where men have never cared to haunt,
nor women have walked with me,
And ghosts then keep their distance;
and I know some liberty.

We are all ghosts in other people's lives.

EMMA
You are a most imaginative woman, Mrs Henniker.

THE OTHER WOMAN
Thank you.

EMMA
It was not intended to be a compliment. It does not do for ladies to have
an active imagination. Do you not think that you might have allowed
yourself to overreach your capacity? The novel you wrote with Thomas
– *The Spectre of the Real*. Was quite … sensational.

THE OTHER WOMAN
We women all have more capacity than the world might expect. I have
written novels of my own as well, you know.

EMMA
Ah, yes, I believe I saw a copy on the station bookstall when we last
went up to Town. In the remaindered section.

THE OTHER WOMAN
I have not seen yours at all as yet.

EMMA
Why no, I have not found the right publisher.

THE OTHER WOMAN
Could Tom not make some introductions?

EMMA
I do not need his patronage. I am, like you, an independent-thinking woman. And there has been so much to do about Max Gate.

THE OTHER WOMAN
Oh, yes, but surely you have more time for yourself? I thought Tom was employing another copyist.

EMMA
Indeed, and I feel that is where things have gone wrong. There has been no-one to watch over the more imaginative aspects of his writing. He is apt to become heated in composition.

THE OTHER WOMAN
He has become more outspoken of late. More direct, should I say. But I found working with him on our novel most stimulating.

EMMA
Stimulation is not required in my writing.

THE OTHER WOMAN
No, you were always more sentimental in your outlook.

EMMA
Thomas's ideas were never *comme il faut*. But of late they have become positively lurid. *Ethelberta* was so slight but the ideas contained therein so inappropriate. The daughter of a butler a great poet! I, on the other hand, used my time in Swanage to greater effect. *The Lady on the Shore* was an immensely superior work.

THE OTHER WOMAN

I was not aware that there was a competitive element to writing novels. Now, Emma, if we are to fall out, I will take my trusty steed and be on my way. 'Withdraw thy foot from thy friend's house lest he weary of thee.'

[She goes to her bicycle. EMMA stops her]

EMMA

Please don't say that. Let us be friends. Tell me something wise and witty. Let us discuss intelligently. I have so few friends.

THE OTHER WOMAN

Has Tom obtained that carriage for you yet?

EMMA

He has been so occupied of late. So many other things on his mind.

THE OTHER WOMAN

My dear, you simply must insist. It will not do for a woman of your standing to be so imprisoned.

EMMA

Imprisoned? That is a harsh word.

THE OTHER WOMAN

But if your husband is against it ...?

EMMA

I did not say that. Merely that he has been preoccupied with that book. And other things ...

THE OTHER WOMAN

But how do you get about? Your leg. He surely must see ...

EMMA

When I raise the matter he appears to listen. To be enthusiastic even. But then in a few minutes his mind is racing ahead and it is gone. Not even a dog cart.

THE OTHER WOMAN
In that case, you must have a bicycle.

EMMA
A bicycle. Oh, no. That would be too undignified for someone of my standing. I mean ... I beg your pardon, I couldn't ...

THE OTHER WOMAN
Nonsense Here, try my machine. He surely couldn't object to a bicycle?

EMMA
I told you. He doesn't object. No, I cannot bring myself to do it. Somehow you are able to carry these things off. You can espouse such modern ideas without compromising your old values.

THE OTHER WOMAN
But first tell me about this parcel. Why are you and your housemaid wrestling over it in such an unseemly manner?

EMMA
This is what I am referring to. *Jude the Obscure*. It is the manuscript of the completed novel. It is worse, far worse than the serial version. It promotes such advanced ideas. Too much for me. Why has he done it? We were so happy once. Seven years we were affectionate. We lived like gypsies; we were poor and moved from home to home. But now he writes about marriage and divorce in such a bitter way. It must be destroyed. Burnt. It should not come before the public. If only he had retained more respect for the old values.

THE OTHER WOMAN
Very well, you spoke of Tom attending university but I'm not sure that would have made any difference to his career. Or his beliefs. For my part, I have no respect for university learning whatever, except, in a qualified degree, on its intellectual side. I had a friend took that out of me. He was the most irreligious man I ever knew, and the most moral. And intellect at Oxford is new wine in old bottles. The mediævalism of Oxford must go, be sloughed off, or Oxford itself will have to go. To be sure, at times one couldn't help having a sneaking liking for the

traditions of the old faith, as preserved by a section of the thinkers there in touching and simple sincerity; but when I was in my saddest, rightest mind I always felt: 'O, ghastly glories of saints, dead limbs of gibbeted Gods! ...'

                              EMMA

Oh, quite so. But one must still attend. On Sunday, at least. Must one not?

                      THE OTHER WOMAN

Must one?

                              EMMA

Does it not behove us to maintain the proprieties? Whatever our beginnings? Which is why this book must be spurned and banished. Have you read it? Of course you have.

                      THE OTHER WOMAN

The wife and the 'other woman'. But which one is which?

                              EMMA

I am the wife, of course.

                      THE OTHER WOMAN

I meant which one is the wife in the book? Which one does God look down on and favour with his blessing? The one he is properly married to in the eyes of the law and divorces? Or the one that loves him but comes to believe that marriage to a divorced man is wrong?

                              EMMA

Now I think you are making fun of me. I have made my feelings on that subject quite clear. I am adamant.

                      THE OTHER WOMAN

Thomas always claims he never bases a character on real life. But we know different, do we not?

EMMA

Do we?

THE OTHER WOMAN

I think we do.

EMMA

Which is why it must be consigned to the flames. It's disgusting.

*[EMMA snatches the book from THE OTHER WOMAN.
She snatches it straight back]*

THE OTHER WOMAN

Book burning. I should leave that for the bishops. They like that sort of thing. Men in power. They love a good bonfire. Warms their cold, dead hearts. They'd all do with a spot of time in Hell right enough. Warm them through thoroughly. Now I believe you promised a cup of tea. And we can investigate this hamper of costumes. And whatever you do, this must not be destroyed.

[She holds the parcel just out of reach]

EMMA

I still intend that it shall not be published. He has gone further ... much further than propriety allows. You and I, we are such friends, are we not? We will not fall out over this, will we?

[EMMA glares at the package THE OTHER WOMAN is holding]

Similar interests and background. Tea, then. Amelia!

[In frustration EMMA exits. THE MOTHER is left asleep on the bench]

THE OTHER WOMAN

Propriety! I am driven by propriety. I am a modern woman. I preach freedom of thought and yet I cannot wrench myself away from what is proper in myself. Dear God, if you exist why do you lead us by such a chain?

[She sings]

Through the clouds of dust I come
On my bicycle. On my bicycle.
Racing forward, racing forward
Into the future, into the future
Putting the past behind me.

Through the Dorset that he knows
Through the Dorset that he knows
I know he loves me, he loves me
But it is not to be, not to be:
A married woman with children.

I want to be a paradigm for other women to show
Show it's possible. It's possible
That it's possible to change
But I am tied
By a jarring faith
That means I must say no.

So I am found on Ingpen Beacon,
or on Wylls-Neck to the west,
Or else on homely Bulbarrow,
or little Pilsdon Crest,

Where men have never cared to haunt,
nor women have walked with me,
And ghosts then keep their distance;
and I know some liberty.

[THE MAID returns to claim the package]

THE MAID
Please, your Ladyship, the Missus says Tea's ready ...

THE OTHER WOMAN
Thank you.

THE MAID
And she says I'm to take that parcel to her.

THE OTHER WOMAN
I'll keep it. For the moment, I think. There, girl, don't look so downcast.
You are allowing your worries to throw you down. You are young. You
must rise up and defeat your cares as Gideon did the Midianites ... You
must buy a bicycle. You must get out into the world and learn all about
it. From the saddle of a bicycle, things look so much better.

[She pushes the bicycle over to THE MAID]

Here. Try it. It could change your life.

THE MAID
Must I?

THE OTHER WOMAN
Indeed you must. Every young woman should.

[THE MAID tries but she cannot manage it]

You are not trying. You let your sex down!

[THE OTHER WOMAN exits. THE MAID sits down and begins to cry]

THE MAID
[As TESS]

*How could I be expected to know? I was a child when I left my house four
months ago. Why didn't you tell me there was danger in men-folk? Why
didn't you warn me? Ladies know what to fend hands against, because
they read novels that tell them of these tricks; but I never had the chance
o' learning in that way, and you did not help me!*

Now how do I get thic blessed parcel back again?

[Exit]

'You are not trying.'

END OF ACT 1

ACT 2

[A little while later. The same part of the garden. THE MOTHER is dozing on her bench. EMMA and THE OTHER WOMAN arrive arm in arm from the house. EMMA scowls at THE MOTHER and then pulls THE OTHER WOMAN to one side]

EMMA

My dear Mrs Henniker, you are my friend, are you not?

THE OTHER WOMAN

Do you doubt it?

EMMA

I can speak to you in confidence?

THE OTHER WOMAN

Of course. Treat me as a sister.

EMMA

This is awkward.

[She motions to the apparently sleeping MOTHER. THE OTHER WOMAN leads her to the other bench where they talk in low whispers]

THE OTHER WOMAN

Go on. Sister.

EMMA

For some time now ... since we moved here ... we have not been happy.

THE OTHER WOMAN

My dear Emma. Why ever not? You have everything that a woman can crave. A new house built by her husband. A successful husband whose income and standing is assured.

EMMA

I fear we have not been happy ... as a man and wife.

THE OTHER WOMAN

Ah! I see. But come, my dear, that is the case with many couples. Particularly those of mature years. It is sometimes better. One can use one's energies in more productive ways. Your writing, for instance. Your love for animals. Your causes. The anti-vivisection league.

EMMA

No. That is not entirely the problem. It is Thomas. He will not speak of it.

THE OTHER WOMAN

Indeed, men find it difficult to put into words what women feel as of nature.

EMMA

Yet, he seems content with the situation. Positively content. You see, what I fear ... He is a man with followers. Adherents, almost. He is surrounded by a mob at times. There are so many who would be close to him.

THE OTHER WOMAN

I see.

EMMA

You are my true friend, are you not?

THE OTHER WOMAN

Of course.

EMMA

And you would tell me if there was a breath ... of indiscretion.

THE OTHER WOMAN

A lover without indiscretion is no lover at all.

EMMA

Mrs Henniker, how could you? How could you make light of such a thing? It hurts me so.

THE OTHER WOMAN

My dear. I am contrite. I only meant to say that had there been the merest whiff of impropriety it would have been noised abroad at once.

EMMA

But have I been blind? Are people laughing at me from behind their handkerchiefs?

THE OTHER WOMAN

There is a condition worse than blindness and that is seeing something that isn't there.

[Exeunt. THE MOTHER opens one eye and then closes it again. THE MAID arrives dressed in a costume with a large hat with feathers]

THE MAID
[Sings]

I left you in tatters, without shoes or socks,
Tired of digging potatoes, and spudding up docks;
And now I've gay bracelets and bright feathers three!
Yes: that's how we dress when we're ruined, you see.

At home in the barton I said 'thee' and 'thou',
And 'thik oon' and 'theäs oon' and ''tother'; but now
My talking quite fits me for high compa-ny!
Some polish is gained with one's ruin, you see.

Bournemouth, Bournemouth
City of sin by the sea
Bournemouth, Bournemouth
It's a sin what you did tor me.

My hands were like paws then, my face blue and bleak
But now you're bewitched by my delicate cheek,
And my little gloves fit as on any la-dy!
We never do work when we're ruined, you see.

46

I used to call home-life a hag-ridden dream,
And I'd sigh, and I'd sock; but at present I seem
To know not of megrims or melancho-ly!
True. One's pretty lively when ruined, you see.

Bournemouth, Bournemouth
City of sin by the sea
Bournemouth, Bournemouth
It's a sin what you did tor me.

THE MAID
[Crosses to the sleeping MOTHER]

You should not have sat here so long, Mrs Hardy. 'Tis September and
not as warm as it was. You'll catch your death.

THE MOTHER
'Tis of no account, my child. I've had a nap while sitting here. Yes, I've
had a nap, and went straight up into my old country again, as usual.
The place was as natural as when I left it, e'en just threescore years ago!
All the folks and my old aunt were there, as when I was a child – yet I
suppose if I were really to set out and go there, hardly a soul would be
left alive to say to me, dog how art? But tell Hannah to stir her stumps
and serve supper – though I'd fain do it myself, the poor old soul is
getting so unhandy! Has that daughter-in-law of mine gone?

THE MAID
She has gone to find Mr Hardy again. And your daughter. I think she
wants them to ... escort you away.

THE MOTHER
Ah, the world is an ungrateful place! 'Twas a pity I didn't take my poor
name off this earthly calendar and creep under ground sixty long years
ago, instead of leaving my own county to come here! But I told him
how 'twould be – marrying so many notches above him. The child was
sure to chaw high, unlike his father!

THE MAID
That woman ...

THE MOTHER

What woman?

THE MAID

The one dressed as a man.

THE MOTHER
[Imitating EMMA]

That is no woman. That is Mrs Henniker. She is the daughter of Lord Houghton. She is a lady.

THE MAID

If you say so.

THE MOTHER

I do say so.

THE MAID

She looks mighty like a man to me. She said I should buy a bicycle. She said it would make me free.

THE MOTHER

The only way you can be free is to save yourself from getting married. You've read *Under the Greenwood Tree*? Fancy Day's father saves up and sends his daughter to training college to learn to be a teacher. Well, I did the same. Saved up so that Mary could go to Salisbury. Years it took me. It wouldn't have been any good if she got married. She's a good'n. Headmistress of her own school. That's what you ought to do. Don't concern yourself with marriage. It'll only hold you back. You'd be as free as a little bird on a branch if only you don't marry.

Did you ever feel this place was haunted?

THE MAID

No. No. Only by the Missus ... she has a weird presence. She shuts herself away in her bedroom in the attic for most of the day but sometimes ... she haunts the house like a ghost.

48

THE MOTHER

When they were digging the well they found a pile of skeletons six foot deep. All piled on top of each other. They come from Roman times so they weren't Christian. That's what they've built her home on. Heathen foundations.

[She says it again louder]

Heathen unnatural foundations this house has.

[THE OTHER WOMAN returns with EMMA. They are carrying costume hats and scripts. EMMA stops. She has heard the last line as she was meant to]

EMMA

What? What did you say? This is a Christian household.

THE OTHER WOMAN

I thought your son had eschewed all that. I thought he had become a humanist. We have had many discussions on the subject. I wish I could agree with him on every point he makes.

EMMA

Humanist he may be but he still accompanies me to church on Sunday.

THE MOTHER

All I was saying was that there were skeletons buried in the garden. They found them when they were building the house.

EMMA

Skeletons? Where?

THE MOTHER

When they was digging the well. Hundreds of them. Their faces all drawn in horror of their dreadful ungodly execution. Heathen sacrifices right on this spot where your roses grow. Horrible to think, baint it?

EMMA

Impossible. I was never told.

THE MOTHER

Ah, no. I think he thought you were of a sensitive nature. It mid upset you. Drive you mad.

EMMA

I would have been told. Mr Hardy tells me everything. We are open with each other. And I'll thank you not to make such slanders.

THE MOTHER

It's not slander if it's the truth, so I believe.

EMMA

How dare you.

THE MOTHER

Well, you best go and ask him. See who's right.

EMMA

Ah, I understand. But I know he has kept nothing from me.

THE OTHER WOMAN

Come, Emma, let us put all that supernatural nonsense to one side. We are, after all, rational modern women, are we not? I think we have enough material here for our little entertainment. You will help us, won't you, Mrs Hardy. And you, Amelia?

THE MAID

I'm supposed to be Tess this afternoon. And I've got to get to the post office. If you would let me have that parcel.

THE OTHER WOMAN

There is plenty of time for that. And this won't take any more of your time. I think you will know the piece off by heart already.

THE MAID

I know Tess because I've read it so many times.

THE MOTHER

I can't read words off a page. My eyesight ...

THE OTHER WOMAN

That's the beauty of this entertainment. I have chosen a moment from *The Return of the Native*.

EMMA

We were so happy when that was written. We had a lovely house overlooking the water meadows at Sturminster. Before Thomas was quite in the public eye and we ... moved here. And you intend that I take part in this ... charade?

THE OTHER WOMAN

I insist. We need at least four of us.

[She picks up the costumes]

We are to portray the part where Eustacia Vye disguises herself as a boy and takes part in the ancient mummers' play. I'm sure you can both remember the lines the mummers recite.

EMMA

Do I assume that you are to take the part of Eustacia?

THE OTHER WOMAN

It would be capital fun: 'the raw material of a divinity whose celestial imperiousness, love, wrath, and fervour had proved to be somewhat thrown away on netherward Egdon.'

EMMA

She disguises herself so that she can get close to a man that she has taken a fancy to whilst discarding another quite callously.

THE MOTHER

'Tis for ploughboys and the like. Not for grown women. We mid lose all our dignities.

EMMA

'As the crackling of thorns under a pot so is the laughter of the fool.'

THE OTHER WOMAN

But that is why it is such an ideal piece. We will all disguise ourselves.
No-one will know who we are.

EMMA

I cannot be seen. Not like this. 'A good name is precious as ointment.'

THE OTHER WOMAN

Come, Emma. It is not the time to be quoting Ecclesiastes. And in any
case your name will not be impugned because you will not be seen. Put
these on ...

*[She hands out paper hats for the mummers' play with paper streamers
veiling their faces]*

... and here are the words.

*[She distributes scripts and paper swords and strikes a pose as
Eustacia Vye]*

'Go ahead, lads, with the try-over. I'll challenge any of you to find a
mistake in me.'

THE MOTHER
[Reluctantly describing the acting area with her stick]

*'Make room, make room, my gallant boys
And give us space to rhyme:
We've come to show Saint George's play
Upon this Christmas time.'*

EMMA

The mummers did come at Christmas but Mr Hardy was at work in his
study. I gave them a shilling and told them to be off. I could hear them
laughing at the door. And later Mr Hardy said he was sorry he missed
them. He had not heard them since he was a child. Such foolishness.

THE OTHER WOMAN
Well, now is your chance to make amends. You can show him what he missed. Here ...

[The next section is a re-enactment of the mummers' play from The Return of The Native, *in which THE OTHER WOMAN takes the part of Eustacia Vye and EMMA that of St George and THE MOTHER as Father Christmas. THE MAID will later become the Doctor]*

EMMA
[Very reluctantly]

'Hear comes I son George from England have I sprung
sum of my worndras works now for to begin
first into a Closat I was put
then into a Cave was lock
I sot my foot upon a Rockhe stone
their did I make my sad an griveus mone
how many men have I slew
and rund the firehe dragon thrue.'

I don't want to do this! It is quite unbecoming. Besides, the meaning is quite unclear.

THE OTHER WOMAN
Nonsense. Let it be a demonstration of your acting abilities. You have so many.

EMMA
'I fought them all Courragesly
and stil got of thire victory
England's right England admorration
now ear I drow my bloody weepon
ho is the man that doth be fore me Stand
I will cut him down with my Courrageus hand.'

Are you quite sure? That this will be quite proper? The language is so ... coarse.

53

The Mummers' Play.

THE OTHER WOMAN

Perfectly!

> *'Hear come's I the Turkish Knight*
> *came from the Turkish land to fight*
> *I will fight sun George that man of Courrage*
> *and if is blood is hot soon will I make it Could.'*

EMMA

> *'Thee come so far a way to fight such man as I,*
> *I will cut thy dublats ful of Hylent hols*
> *and make thy buttens fly.'*

What did you mean about 'acting abilities'?

THE OTHER WOMAN

Flexibilities, I meant. You have the capacity for the same sort of imagination that great actresses have. You are a true romantic. You can imagine yourself into any one of a number of situations. And you have the power to imagine away all the bad and immoral things that surround you.

'I am a man of vallour I will fight untill I die
sun George thou never will face me but away from me will fly.'

EMMA
'Ha proud Turk what wilt will thou tell me so
with threting words and threting oath's
drow thy sord and fight drow thy pus and pay
for satisfaction I will have be fore I go a way.'

You have come here just to see that man. You hussy!

THE OTHER WOMAN
[Out of character]

What man? What are you ...

[She suddenly realises that EMMA is speaking to her as Eustacia Vye]

Oh, I see.

[Back in character]

But I am so bored. I must have stimulation.

[She bursts into peals of laughter]

'No satisfaction shall you have
but in a moment's time I will bring thee to thy grave.'

EMMA
'Thee bring me to my grave?
I will fight with thee
no pardon shall you have
so drow thy sord and fight
for I will Concour you this night.'

[Suddenly realising the others are all sniggering at her efforts]

55

You are all making fun of me. I won't have it. In my own garden.

THE OTHER WOMAN
Oh, Emma. You are delicious! Then you hit me with the sword.

[EMMA makes a tentative prod]

Not like that. Give it a hearty swipe.

EMMA
I am not a Grimaldi. This is not a harlequinade.

THE OTHER WOMAN
Harder. Harder. Mrs Hardy.

[Now everyone is laughing out loud]

EMMA
I want to be taken seriously.

*[She swipes THE OTHER WOMAN hard with her sword. THE OTHER
WOMAN collapses heavily to the ground]*

Good God, I've killed her. Are you all right? Have I hurt you?

THE MOTHER
*'As i gist stiping out of my bed
in hearing this my honly son was dead
o cruel christan what ast thou don
thou ast ruin'd me and killed my only son.'*

EMMA
You stupid woman. Stop playing. Can't you see that Mrs Henniker is
hurt?

THE MAID
It's all right, Madam. I think I can cure him, her.

EMMA

Did you not hear? Mrs Henniker is hurt. You, girl, don't stand there like Patience on a monument. Go and get help. Find a doctor. Get some smelling salts.

[The following speeches overlap in a generally growing level of confusion]

Mrs Henniker. Mrs Henniker!

THE MAID
'i can cure the hich the stich the pox the gout
all deses and comnpleases
if any man as got a scolin wife
my balsom will her cure
take but one drap of this upon my life
she will never scoal no more.'

EMMA

What do you know about doctoring? Have you some sal volatile? Fetch Mr Hardy. At once.

[THE OTHER WOMAN begins to move]

I think she's coming round. I think she's all right.

THE OTHER WOMAN
'What places is are?
what seens appare
whare ever itorn mine eye
tis all around in chantin ground
and soft delusions rise.'

EMMA

Lie still. Lie still. You are quite delirious.

THE OTHER WOMAN
[Suddenly springing to her feet]

Not at all. You see. Perfectly fit and well. I am quite cured.

57

EMMA

Oh, thank God. Are you really all right? No headache at all?

THE OTHER WOMAN

None at all. You see, my dear, I was acting. The Turkish Knight slain by St George.

[The others burst out laughing]

EMMA

Of all the tricks. I thought ...

THE OTHER WOMAN

'o pardon pardon St George one thing of thee icrav
spair me my life and i will be thy constant slave.'

EMMA

Stop it. Stop it all of you. You are laughing at me. All of you. I will not be mocked. Well, you, Mrs Hardy, I might not have expected any better. But you, Mrs Henniker. I am ashamed of you. You are a disgrace to your class. And I am made to look a fool in front of my maid-servant.

THE OTHER WOMAN

Come now, Emma. Do not fret so. Let us go and surprise Thomas with our little play. He will be delighted.

EMMA

I will not. I will not be seen in the company of my maid and that woman.

THE OTHER WOMAN

The feast of misrule. It is Christmas after all and *noblesse oblige*.

EMMA

But it's not Christmas. I can't imagine why she has come here at all today if it is not to make fun of me.

THE MOTHER

Can't a mother come to see her own son? Would you keep that from me?

EMMA

You have never been here before. You could have gone over to see him any time but you remained here. To annoy me. You have come specifically to show me up when all the neighbours were here.

THE MOTHER

I am sorry I'm such a disgrace to you. I know I am only the mother to your husband. You were always one to chaw high.

EMMA

We may not be of the same class but you are still a disgrace to all our sex. Perhaps you thought that because you were the mother of my husband that you had a right to command me. But that is not so. All our married life you have tried to set him against me. Well, if it wasn't for me he would not have achieved anything. I have given him everything.

THE MOTHER

You brought Tom neither youth nor wealth, small intelligence and no children.

EMMA

How dare you!

THE OTHER WOMAN

Come, Emma. Let us not become heated.

EMMA

This has been going on too long. It must be settled. You think I don't know what you're talking about behind my back with your quaint dialect. But I know what you're saying. I know what you mean when you say I 'chaw high'. Indeed. Well, it's not me that 'chaws high', it is you. You've always mocked me or my lameness and for my beliefs and for my speech but I am not mocked. Despite my superior social position you have looked down on me from your charming rustic tower. You've sought to shut me out from your society as if I was not good enough for you. And you and your family have tried to interfere – to come between a man and a wife. Don't think I don't know what has been said. What you say to Tom. I know what you think about our lack of children. But those are not matters that can concern you. If it was for you Tom would never have married at all. There would have been no prospect at all of that which perhaps you hold so dear.

It was I who recognised his talent. Persuaded him to give up architecture. Supported him through all our vicissitudes. I opened the door to his talent. And yet you still sneer. Well, no more. You will not come here again spreading your poison. I am going to be *the* Mrs Hardy from now on and I will make sure that we are together as a man and wife should be.

THE MOTHER
You couldn't keep a man at your side. My husband wasn't much in that way but at least I made sure that he never strayed.

[Silence]

EMMA
[In a cold fury]

Now you better go. Go on and don't ever let me see you here again.

THE MOTHER
I knew you were excitable ...

EMMA
Excitable!

THE MOTHER
But I didn't know that you were completely mad.

'Don't ever let me see you here again.'

EMMA

What? Mad! You are a witch-like creature and quite equal to any amount of evil-wishing and speaking – I can imagine you and your daughters on your native heath raising a storm on Walpurgis night. Why did you come here, any of you, if not to torment me? To drive me mad.

[EMMA makes to leave]

THE OTHER WOMAN

Emma ... Sister.

[EMMA looks at her with a new-found awareness and then turns and goes]

THE MAID

I think that was a cruel act and I'm sorry I took part in it. I think you are both ... begging your pardon ...

THE OTHER WOMAN

You may as well say your piece. Speak your mind. You should be free to have your say as well.

THE MAID

Very well. I'll tell you about freedom. All your talk of freedom for women, your bicycling. I'll tell what freedom like that means for such as me. If I go out for the day picnicking in the countryside on one of those, who looks after baby? A mother's duty is to her child. It has to be fed, poor little milky thing. It has to have shelter from the rain.

When I was seventeen, I'd read books. I thought I could better myself. I wasn't like Tess. I told myself I wasn't going to make the same mistakes as she did. It wasn't fate that drove me to leave home, it was my own choice. My own free will. My own foolishness. I did what you thought girls should do, Mrs Hardy, I tried to better myself. And what did I get for my pains? The same as all girls do who try that road – a baby and a life of being passed by in the street. Your talk of freedom is all false. There baint no freedom for such as I and never will be.

And would I be better off getting married than not? The answer is that if anyone would have me and the baby, I'd take him without a thought. I tried the other way and 'tisn't in a man's nature to look after his child unless you have him tied close. But would any man have me now? Probably not. Where's my future and freedom?

And now you've used me to undermine my mistress who is in a precarious state of mind as it is. You've made sideways comments about Mrs Hardy all afternoon. Well, I might despise her for her odd ways and her condescension, but she took me in when others sent me packing. There are those who would have as soon seen me hanged as give me charity. She is a Christian woman to that extent and she is kinder than a lot of supposed free-thinking people.

And the tragedy is that all these visitors, they don't come to see the Missus. Although she thinks they do. Even her special friends laugh at her behind her back and they push past her as soon as they can to talk to the Great Man himself.

I'm sorry I've spoken like that. I know I should have kept respectful like but you made me speak and now I've said more than I ought.

[THE OTHER WOMAN goes to speak but is unable to do so. She turns the package over in her hands. She moves to leave]

THE OTHER WOMAN

Propriety!

[She leaves. The package remains on the bench]

THE MOTHER

I only wanted him to be happy. It's all a mother wants. I wanted for him what I couldn't have myself. Perhaps she did him a good turn, not having children. Eh? Do you think so?

I'm feeling faint, my dear. Could you fetch me a cup of water?

[THE MAID leaves]

Why, there's a little patch of shepherd's thyme by the path. 'Tis so perfumed. And a little throng of ants crossing. A never-ending, heavy-laden throng. They will have been here long before the house was built. Crossing that patch of thyme. Long before the Romans. Back and forth. I can see them over there on the lawn clustered around Tom just like the ants. Back and forth they go. Back and forth. Careless of me. That wife of his, that Other Woman. What it is to be old and forgotten. Is that a mother's lot in the end? To be cast off by her son? I came all this way on Mary's arm and I never spoke to him after all.

[THE MAID returns with a cup]

THE MAID

Here, drink this.

[THE MOTHER sips]

Come, we'll find Mary in the throng and I'll see you to the gate.

THE MOTHER

I don't like this house. Never did. It's too four-square. And him an architect with proper certificates. It's not his style. And it's haunted. All those skeletons in the ground and witches flying around the chimney pots.

THE MAID
Do you want me to say anything to Madam?

THE MOTHER
Tell her you have seen a broken-hearted woman cast off by her son.

[Exeunt. EMMA watches them go. She picks up the manuscript]

EMMA
There they go to join the mass, all clustered around him. The Great Man. His family, his admirers and sycophants. He's never taken my side. Never spoken for me. I know they're talking about me. And now they mock me. Laughing at me. Ah, there's Mrs Henniker. Standing next to him where I should be. Oh, my God. I have been blind. Mrs Henniker.

Not only blind but stupid.

[Sings]

There have always been ghosts
That have lived in my mind
Of the things that I've lost
Things left behind.
There have always been thoughts
When I stop on the stair
To listen to voices
When there's nobody there.

The voice of my talent
A voice still unheard
So tricky to handle
Like a little caged bird.

The ghost of my longing
And the shades of self scorn

64

The waste of my womanhood
And the children unborn.

The ghost of my marriage
And a love that's long lost
Like the brown leaves of autumn
And the long winter frost.

The ghost of belief
That's been certain and sure
Is crumbling around me
Like the cliffs on the shore.

There have always been ghosts
That have lived in my mind
Of the things that I've lost
Things left behind.
There have always been thoughts
When I stop on the stair
To listen to voices
When there's nobody there.

[THE MAID comes back]

THE MAID

Please, Missus, Mr Hardy ... the others, they want you to go and join them. Mr Hardy, he particular wants you to be with him. He says he can't do anything till you come.

EMMA

Who said that?

THE MAID

Mr Hardy. He's got a seat for you. Right in the middle. Between him and Mrs Henniker. They can't start without you. I'll tell them you're coming. Shall I?

'There have always been ghosts.'

EMMA
Mrs Henniker? You know I opened the door to her. She was my friend.

THE MAID
Yes, Missus, you did ...

EMMA
When we were first married we wandered about like tramps. We moved
from house to house. Bournemouth, Swanage, Yeovil, Sturminster
Newton, London. I had nothing. No possessions. But I was the one who
supported him, did all the work copying the novels by candlelight until
my eyes were red and strained. I even wrote some of the novels – *Under
the Greenwood Tree*, that's mine. We worked together. Man and wife. It
didn't matter who wrote what. They belonged to both of us. And, for a
while I thought we were happy. We were happy.

Now I look back and realise what we've done without ... a home,
children. That's what makes them so poisonous. In the end, there is
nothing to show for it.

THE MAID
But there have been children ... The books, I mean. Aren't they the
offspring to your marriage? And you wouldn't want the other type
anyhow, mucky, milky little things.

EMMA
I shan't live like this. I shan't. Why didn't he build me a proper house
with proper gardens? I shouldn't have to live in a suburban brick box at
the side of a turnpike. Not with these skeletons to haunt me. And the
light cut out by all those trees. I deserve better. I shan't be a laughing
stock to my friends any more.

But I'll show them. I'll make sure they look up to me in my proper
place. I will burn that book. Then there will be room for my work to
grow and be noticed.

At least they are gone. Those women. Good riddance, I say. They won't
step foot here again. Not whilst I'm alive. His mother. It's insufferable
that I should have to be polite to such a woman. And her gruesome
daughters. That ... minnow, Mary, and that crow, Kate. They won't drag
me down any more. Or her. It's insufferable.

I have given him everything. I gave him all my love and he grew tired of it.

I can't even visit respectable friends. He won't let me have my own carriage. I'm no more than a prisoner. I won't endure it. I want to be able to hold my head up. There'll be no more books. Not like that one. Go ahead and publish it, Tom. But that will be the last. I should have kept up the copying. That's my fault, I suppose. I should have been keeping an eye. Making sure it was up to the standard I've come to expect. Well, no more. We're not going to become dragged down by such obscenities.

THE MAID

I'll go and tell them, then.

[THE MAID hovers uncertainly. She sees the parcel and picks it up]

Then I'll go straight to the post office.

[EMMA turns and snatches the parcel from her]

EMMA

I'll finish my novel and then we shall see who's the better writer. I have devoted my life to his writing. Given myself heart and soul. And, to my shame, I have let my own talent slide. Well, we'll see about that. There are those who know. Those who know what it is to be cast into the shadow of a husband. Well, the world turns on and I will be recognised.

And I'll show them who is the modern woman. An independent woman. Even without a carriage. I shall obtain a bicycle. Yes. Modern women ride bicycles.

[She wheels the bicycle to the centre of the lawn]

That may be my way out to freedom. I can ride into town. Visit. Go on picnics. We did before and we shall again. Yes. And Tom shall have a bicycle, too. We shall be seen out. A respectable modern couple. We shan't travel by omnibus as we had to when we visited Corfe Castle.

'He will love me again.'

[She hands the parcel to THE MAID who stands watching. During the following she tries and fails several times to mount the cycle and ride it until she manages to circle the lawn]

It will be as I was in Cornwall all those years ago. Instead of a horse, I shall have a bicycle. And perhaps ... We shall ride together as we did then. He will woo me anew from the saddle of his bicycle. We shall begin again. But this time as a respectable married couple. And me a modern woman. He will love me again. On our bicycles.

[THE MAID holds out the parcel to her]

Don't bother me with that now, girl. Didn't Mr Hardy tell you to take it to the post? Well, hurry up or you'll miss the entertainment.

[THE MAID turns and hurries out with the package]

Thomas! Thomas! Don't start without me.

[And she cycles unsteadily off]

THE END

The curtain call.

Afterword –
Writing She Opened the Door

The historical context – 1895

Although I make few references to the world outside the Max Gate garden in the script, for a writer it is vitally important to know something about the period that he is trying to describe. Language, manners, costumes, all are part of the historical context and affect the way in which characters talk and interact. They have to be absorbed thoroughly. On the other hand, a writer doesn't wish to create a pastiche nor yet to appear too heavy-handed with the research. The period has to be easy to understand and accessible to a contemporary audience that may not have the historical background in their heads. It is the writer's job to have that context.

The biographies written by proper writers will provide accounts of what Thomas and Emma were up to at this time so I defer to them for an accurate description of events, but, for the sake of completeness, I'll just give a brief outline of what was happening in the rest of the world during 1895.

Many of the events of this year, we may suppose, would have provided topics for heated discussion over the breakfast table (Emma had not yet retreated to the isolation of her attic room). A bitter winter must have concerned them both as Max Gate was notoriously cold, but perhaps they would be pleased that pests in the garden would have been reduced by the vicious frosts, even if it chilled the little wild animals that they would both have cared about. I'm sure Emma would have put out more than breadcrumbs for the birds on frosty days. The General Election that occurred in July must have caused some upset. The Liberals under Lord Rosebery lost to the Conservative Lord Salisbury. I think we can imagine that Thomas and Emma would have been at odds over that result. Earlier in the year the National Trust had come into being. The Hardys may or may not have been aware of it at that time, but as Thomas was an enthusiastic supporter of the Society for the Protection of Ancient Buildings it would have been an ideal close to their hearts.

But the most controversial topic of the year would have been the doings of Oscar Wilde. From the heady heights of the success of *The Importance of Being Earnest* in February to the events at the Cadogan Hotel and his eventual imprisonment in Reading Gaol, his was a saga that played out over the year. Thomas and Emma must have been shaken by the news whether they were in sympathy or not.

Abroad there had been the Dreyfus affair in France, the end of the Sino-Japanese war and, of especial interest perhaps to characters in our play, news from Munich that bicyclists would have to pass a test before venturing out onto a public highway.

Bicycling

The Safety bicycle was invented in 1885 and was soon seized on by feminists and suffragists as a way of providing freedom for women. As mass production took hold and the machines became cheaper, even the

In Dorsetshire. Fair Cyclist: 'Is this the way to Wareham, please?' Native: 'Yes, Miss, yew seem to me to ha' got 'em on all right!' (Reproduced with permission of Punch Ltd, www.punch.co.uk.)

lower classes were able to escape some of the drudgery of their lives. Susan B. Anthony, the American advocate of civil rights and women's suffrage, said: 'Let me tell you what I think of bicycling. I think it has done more to emancipate women than anything else in the world. It gives women a feeling of freedom and self-reliance. I stand and rejoice every time I see a woman ride by on a wheel ... the picture of free, untrammeled womanhood.' Bicycling was seen as healthful and spiritually uplifting and even ladies like Florence Henniker could be caught up in the craze. In reality it was probably not Florence Henniker who introduced the Hardys to bicycling but their friends Hamo and Agatha Thornycroft, but the general sentiment is the same.

The bicycle craze in the 1890s also helped liberate women from corsets and ankle-length skirts and other restrictive garments by substituting startling divided skirts and bloomers. To show just how far this reached into the national consciousness is illustrated by the number of cartoons that magazines like *Punch* carried of women wearing so-called 'Rational Dress'.

Hardy and women

One of the perceived contradictions in the literature of Thomas Hardy is his attitude to women. There are any number of accounts of his apparent misogyny and how it was demonstrated in his attitude towards his heroines. To me, this seems to be utterly nonsensical. From the variety of types and individuals of women in his books it is clear that he must have been a great observer of women and had a good deal of understanding of how they function and what drives them. On top of that is his tendency to place women at the centre of his narrative. The women may be buffeted by circumstance and events beyond their control but they all seem to be the ones on whose decisions the narrative hangs. In *The Mayor of Casterbridge*, for instance, it is Susan's decision to go with the sailor and try to find a better way of life for her and her daughter that is the narrative spring that gives Henchard the impetus to set off to better himself. And it is her return that triggers his undoing. Hardy gives space to Susan to argue her case and, to a modern reader, her actions are entirely defensible.

'Mike,' she said, 'I've lived with thee a couple of years, and had nothing but temper! Now I'm no more to 'ee; I'll try my luck elsewhere. 'Twill be better for me and Elizabeth-Jane, both. So good-bye!'

The same could be said to apply to Tess; circumstance is against her but she does at least make some of the brave decisions which lead to her own downfall. Hardy allows, and indeed encourages, complexity in his characters. Just because a character makes a bad decision doesn't mean the writer thinks of her as a bad person or feels antipathy towards her. More than this, Hardy's women seem often to be forceful – actual forces of nature – for instance, Eustacia Vye and Arabella Donn. One only has to compare Hardy's work with say Dickens, whose only women characters are mere walk-ons, cyphers and grotesques, to see how much credibility and power Hardy gave to his women characters.

Despite some bickering with Emma about women's suffrage, which probably had more to do with their personal relationship and his confusion about Florence Henniker, Hardy made it clear in a letter to Millicent Garrett Fawcett, the women's suffrage leader, that he had long been in favour of women's suffrage.

What I learned about the characters

I must emphasise that this play is not a work of scholarship, it is a fantasy. A biographer discovers his or her characters from long hours of research in dusty libraries; a playwright finds them out by writing the play and seeing it performed. The playwright's only concern is that the characters are consistent, credible and react in accordance with the circumstances that are thrown at them.

Having said that, I did immerse myself in a number of the biographies, scholarly works and monographs about the Great Man and those who surrounded him. But, as writers are enjoined to do, I read thoroughly and then threw the research aside and wrote what I felt needed to be written.

I was also more than fortunate to be writing this whilst living in Hardy Country. It is extraordinary the number of people who have a family connection with someone who knew Hardy and Emma. This would never be of any use to a serious biographer but somehow it does provide a sort of inkling of what the truth may have been. Sometimes in these folk memories I might just catch a whiff of the character, like a distant scent of a garden bonfire. In doing so, I may have stumbled upon some truths about the characters of the play that biographers may have overlooked. I hope this is true about Emma, to whom scholars have generally been less than positive.

Emma

Words like snobbish, eccentric and even mad have been bandied around for too long. In constructing a character that is consistent with the facts I managed to uncover, I hope I may have found something in Emma that is a little less hard, a little more deserving of sympathy.

I was shocked when the first piece of scholarship I came across was a long and reasoned piece by Robert Alan Frizzell, suggesting that Emma's madness was the result of tertiary syphilis contracted from Thomas. Although this theory is largely rubbished by other biographers it does give an indication that her behaviour was a long way beyond mere eccentricity. I found a tiny monograph in the Swanage library of someone who, as a small girl, had been taken by Emma for a day out in Bournemouth. There Emma had visited a friend and gone home on the train quite forgetting her small charge. Mad, a medical case or merely forgetful?

I started with the assumption that she was mad in a way that might have some medical foundation but in rehearsal we discovered something marvellous. The character began to talk to us. This was a woman of a certain age (as the Victorians would have put it) – alone in Dorset, cut off from the society she felt she was rightfully part of, and continually reminded of a lower-class family that she felt she had been tricked into joining by marriage. And, above all, there was the constant thronging mass of Thomas's admirers aggravating her disappointment and bitterness that her own efforts at literature and, as she saw it, her contributions to her husband's success were so overlooked. No wonder there had been plate throwing and shouted arguments over the dinner table. As the words were spoken by the actress Jane McKell we began to feel great sympathy for Emma and her predicament. Mad or menopausal?

Then there was the whole question of the relationship with her mother-

Emma Hardy in her middle years. (By permission of the Dorset History Centre.)

in-law which I talk about below. Add to that her undoubted sensitivity about her lameness and her lack of children in an age when motherhood was of importance to a woman and you have a woman who must have trailed bitterness, disappointment and wretchedness everywhere she went – traits that Thomas, with his strong bonds to his mother and family, probably would not have been able to deal with. No wonder he retreated to his study and then, out of remorse for his inability to sympathise, wrote so much about Emma after her death. Mad or misunderstood?

The Other Woman

I acknowledge I was unfair to Florence Henniker in the play. I have deliberately parodied and mixed her up with other real-life characters who surrounded Hardy (which, in defence, is why I call her 'The Other Woman'). I borrowed a great deal of her from Hardy's own works. Mrs Marchmill in *Life's Little Ironies* is supposed to be based on her, so by borrowing from that source, fact and fiction were already folded one on top of another. However, I think I got in all the crucial positive ideas that she carried with her in life: the early forms of feminism and suffragism, her enthusiasm for bicycling and, above all, her intelligence locked in by the necessity of not upsetting

Florence Henniker, the Honourable Mrs Arthur Henniker, daughter of Lord Houghton and Lady Crewe. (By permission of the Dorset History Centre.)

the status quo. She has a comfortable life that she wishes to preserve for the sake of her children. For all her bicycling she cannot embrace the freedom that she enjoins others to enjoy. Her slogan becomes an anguished cry of 'Propriety!'

The Mother

'The Mother' again is a conflation of a number of the Hardy family characters, including the grandmother and the sisters, but this was less about parody and more to indicate the pressures Emma must have felt from the family living just across the water meadows.

The relationship between Emma and her mother-in-law was as fraught as these relationships are prone to be and I believe there is a solid underlying truth in the relationship I portray. In all the time Thomas and Emma were living in Dorchester (before Max Gate was built) Thomas's mother only visited them once and, as far as the record goes, she may never have visited Max Gate at all. Yet Thomas would walk across the water meadows to his old family home most weekends when in Dorset. You can see a picture emerging here. It's clear that Thomas was his mother's boy. His mother was a powerful matriarch with a husband who worked hard but clearly liked time away from the house, drifting through the forest with his own thoughts. Jemima had obviously been frugal with money for she had managed to save enough to send Mary to college, an extraordinary undertaking in itself. She was a woman who had had to be strong and who had impressed upon her children the need for education and learning and independence. She had read *Paradise Lost* and the great works of literature. She must have been a formidable woman who exerted a strong grip on her favourite son even after his marriage. Yet for all these strong points she had one thing against her as far as Emma was concerned: she was from the labouring, albeit skilled, artisan class. This must have rankled Emma beyond measure. Here was a woman to whom she should have shown deference as the mother of her husband but who she considered far beneath her. What's more, Jemima Hardy would have had status in the locality as the rightful Mrs Hardy and every time Emma visited the town she would have been referred to as 'the Other Mrs Hardy'.

Jemima Hardy. (By permission of the Dorset History Centre.)

The Maid

The character of Amelia, 'The Maid', is entirely made up, although I have used her as a vehicle for a view on Tess and other young females who exist in Hardy's works.

I also borrowed from several accounts of the young women that Thomas may have known, Tryphena Sparks, for instance, and a young woman he is said to have met in the Cremorne Gardens in London. This is where Hardy himself is supposed to have drawn inspiration for Tess. The maid is a representational character but I wanted to give her something extra – the beginning of an education. She says (as did Tess) that she passed Sixth Standard at National School, so, who knows, she may have been able to use that to improve her condition. Unlike Tess she is a pragmatist and, I get the feeling, a survivor. If she hadn't been destroyed by child-rearing and poverty she might have been at the height of her powers in the 1920s. While Mrs Henniker would never be able to move the cause of suffragism forward by the necessity of 'propriety', Amelia just may have made it to the ballot box.

By chance, at a performance of the play in Weymouth I happened to meet the great niece of the woman who was the Hardys' maid in real life. Her recollections came too late for me to be able to include but they did give me some reassurance that what I had written about the Hardy household was not a million miles from the truth.

Thomas Hardy himself

I have always been impressed by the many versions there are of Hardy's character – as many as there are biographies, I suppose. And I was struck by the ones that described him as 'grey and invisible'. So I thought the way to see him in the play was to make him entirely invisible and seen only through the eyes of those who surround him. In the play everything revolves around him but he never actually appears. The audience is left to construct their own version of the Man.

But one aspect I did want to draw out and that is the contrast to the generally held view promoted by the Hardy tourist industry that he was living some sort of rural idyll whilst playing the fiddle, sitting on a truss of hay and quaffing a pint of Eldridge Pope's finest. Nothing could be further from the truth.

Hardy was a man of larger society. He and Emma spent four months of the year in London or travelling. He visited the capitals of Europe and talked to the great writers and artists. He attended the opera, he was received in the great salons, he went to those challenging and difficult dramas that were emerging from the pens of playwrights such as Ibsen. He was himself a man lauded and sought after by the establishment, however much he railed against it. His society was not that of rural Dorset but of the educated High Victorian Middle Class. He discussed feminism, vegetarianism, social responsibility and what we would call Green issues. If you want to see what it was that Thomas Hardy thought about society in detail, then read his short stories. Here we begin to see how his thinking was being shaped by the wider society that he was part of and, possibly, where we see a record of that long platonic affair with Florence Henniker.

Dorset for Hardy became a recreation – a place where he could go and live simply with Emma; where they could garden, argue and, later, cycle; where he could play the fiddle and be with family and friends; and where he could write. But the old Dorset he wrote about no longer existed and he knew it. And if he scowled at unannounced visitors and planted trees and built a wall to keep away the long procession of gawpers then I don't blame him.

So what was it that was the contemporary issue that drove Hardy to write? Again, scholars can debate this but I suggest that the principal driving force was the iniquity of the stifling social hierarchy. Hardy had battled with this most of his life. It was a chord played by his mother and grandmother that he should be free of social restraint. It resonates through his work – the place of women, the place of the poor, even the place of the middle class – stratified and boxed so that the whole country was steadily suffocating under its malign influence.

Above all, it was a tune sung by Emma throughout their marriage. She was acutely class conscious and thereby confused and bewildered as to her place in a regulated society as the daughter of gentry, wife of a self-made man and daughter-in-law (as she saw it) of a common labourer. All of this must have underlined their arguments about religion and proper behaviour like a nagging toothache. Emma's view of society pushed him and pulled him until he must have come to despise it.

The novels, at least the great ones, were written about people and events of at least a generation before. *Tess* is set at least 20 years in the past, probably more. Even *Jude* is set some years before the date of writing. No, in these novels, Hardy was deliberately writing about the past. For me, this was because he was writing about themes, big contemporary themes, that he could not confront in a strictly contemporary setting. Having found his fantasy world in rural Wessex in the early novels he realised that he could guide his audience towards discussing bigger and more difficult issues from this viewpoint. Within the apparently exotic location of rural Wessex Hardy was able to examine and mock this evil of social restraint and present it at an objective distance. Hardy was both an outsider and an insider with the unique insight that this gave. If you want evidence, than read *Tess* again and consider the following passage:

> *Clare slowed the horse. He was incensed against his fate, bitterly disposed towards social ordinances; for they had cooped him up in a corner, out of which there was no legitimate pathway. Why not be revenged on society by shaping his future domesticities loosely, instead of kissing the pedagogic rod of convention in this ensnaring manner?*

Angel runs the idea of 'fate' and 'social ordinances' together, as I suggest Hardy himself did. Thus the great phrase at the end of the novel:

> *Justice was done, and the President of the Immortals, in Aeschylean phrase, had ended his sport with Tess.*

This is not Hardy bowing before some superstitious ancient view of fate. He had long ago eschewed a belief in religions of any sort. But here he is describing the strict and overbearing rules of a society that had become a force in itself, crushing those who opposed it and flipping aside any that did not adhere to its binding rule. Throughout his works, replace the idea of 'fate' with that of 'society' and you'll see what I mean. In addition, when Hardy describes Tess as 'a pure woman' he is suggesting not a simple chastity but someone who is untainted by the stink of hypocrisy that such a society engenders. Like Hardy, Tess is an outsider and a simple person who, by circumstance and will, finds herself wandering in this strange garden and wishes only to find the door in the wall that leads out of it.

It would seem that Hardy, having written *Jude*, had ended his own sport with society at large and decided to give up. Well, not quite. This is the time of the great rewriting and reordering – when he has able to revisit many of his great and lesser works that had been edited for propriety. Here he was being more and more open about his feelings. Rather than *Jude* being an endpoint, a dam on the river of his social conscience, it was a floodgate which was opened by the furore surrounding that last novel and which enabled him to reinterpret much of his earlier work in a way that was more honest and straightforward.

It was also a flood that puts Hardy in the first rank because it forms the channel to the modernist writers of the twentieth century and which inspired others such as D.H. Lawrence and Virginia Woolf who were to follow.

Thomas Hardy, the playwright

I never had any qualms about adapting Hardy's novels for the theatre. We all know that he adapted many of them himself, and sanctioned adaptations by others for the stage and the cinema. Indeed, the original Hardy Players performed under his guidance in the garden of Max Gate. Hardy loved the theatre and during his sojourns in London and the cultural hot-spots of Europe he was a great attender of performances at the theatre and the opera. He was friends with the stars of the theatre world and entertained many at Max Gate. Let's not forget, he was a performer himself, playing his fiddle for others to hear, so he had an instinctive understanding of how audiences reacted to performance as opposed to literature.

The novels do present some problems to the adapter, however. The sweep of the Wessex landscape and the way it reflects sentiment and emotion is a tricky thing. Moreover, the authorial voice doesn't always play naturally. However, the richness of characters and the way their stories play out is a joy. Hardy does have a dramatic instinct which leads him to select scenes and dialogue which can be used almost directly. Many of the scenes are told through dazzling dialogue and interaction of character. From *Tess*:

The Hardy Players at Max Gate performing the Mummers' Play from The Return of the Native – *the same piece that I use in* She Opened the Door *Act 2. (By permission of the Dorset History Centre.)*

'Pooh! Well, if you didn't wish to come to Trantridge why did you come?'

She did not reply.

'You didn't come for love of me, that I'll swear.'

''Tis quite true. If I had gone for love o' you, if I had ever sincerely loved you, if I loved you still, I should not so loathe and hate myself for my weakness as I do now! ... My eyes were dazed by you for a little, and that was all.'

He shrugged his shoulders. She resumed –

'I didn't understand your meaning till it was too late.'

'That's what every woman says.'

'How can you dare to use such words!' she cried, turning impetuously upon him, her eyes flashing as the latent spirit (of which he was to see more some day) awoke in her. 'My God! I could knock you out of the gig! Did it never strike your mind that what every woman says some women may feel?'

'Very well,' he said, laughing; 'I am sorry to wound you. I did wrong – I admit it.' He dropped into some little bitterness as he continued: 'Only you needn't be so everlastingly flinging it in my face. I am ready to pay to the uttermost farthing. You know you need not work in the fields or the dairies again. You know you may clothe yourself with the best, instead of in the bald plain way you have lately affected, as if you couldn't get a ribbon more than you earn.'

Her lip lifted slightly, though there was little scorn, as a rule, in her large and impulsive nature.

'I have said I will not take anything more from you, and I will not – I cannot! I SHOULD be your creature to go on doing that, and I won't!'

Above all are the wonderful *coups de théâtre*, switches of fortune and coincidence which, I believe, actually work better on the stage than on the page.

The songs

The songs in *She Opened the Door* were meant to stand as soliloquies in which the characters reveal parts of their inner feelings that would not otherwise become apparent through dialogue. The words are partly Hardy's and partly mine. The first verse of the Mother's song is taken from a Hardy poem *Domicilium*. It was clearly never intended as a lyric but I adapted it and then went on to construct two further verses of my own.

With the Other Woman's song I took the chorus from Hardy (*Wessex Heights*) and wrote the verses to suit the character's inner turmoil. The Maid's song is obviously *The Ruin'd Maid*, slightly adapted to be sung in the first person. I enjoyed writing the chorus and (unlike Hardy) using Bournemouth as the butt of the joke. Emma's song at the end was inspired by *The Ghost of the Past* and one or two other poems that Hardy wrote after Emma's death. However, I have reversed the point of view to that of Emma herself and it becomes a sort of answer to what Hardy will write later.

I was extremely lucky to be able to call upon Roderick Skeaping to compose the music. I wanted music that would reflect my view of Hardy. That is, Thomas Hardy the international figure living squarely in his time, not the throwback folk fiddler. Accordingly, Roderick composed a series of tunes that reflected some of the popular styles of the 1890s. There is a quadrille for the Mother's song that would still have been heard in great dances in the Corn Exchange, there is the Gilbert and Sullivan inspired *Bicycle* song of the Other Woman, the seaside entertainment tune for the Maid and the sentimental drawing-room ballad for Emma's own number.

Fitting it all together

One of the most taxing parts of the writing process was dovetailing the fictional with the factual. I felt the only way I could be free to invent was if I kept as closely as I could to the facts as I understood them. There is nothing unusual in that; most fiction that deals with factual characters sets out to do that. However, where I felt constrained by this was the fact that Thomas and Emma had many years together after the time that this play is set. Consequently, I couldn't invent some grand dramatic ending for the play that wouldn't sit with what we know to have happened afterwards. So I set myself the task of working backwards from the ending. In other words, I realised that there were fascinating aspects of their relationship that were the result of events or circumstances that came about around this time. It felt to me that this general period, the publishing of the final version of *Jude the Obscure*, appeared to change their relationship and I felt I could draw these changes together as strands of the invented narrative.

For instance, consider the bicycling. I had heard accounts of Emma's bicycling down High West Street in Dorchester in a bright blue knickerbocker suit and all the children running after her. And I had read accounts of her and Hardy riding together into the country later. So I think it was quite reasonable to assume that events around this time led to some sort of new beginning – with Emma's new-found love of bicycling and understanding of the idea of personal freedom as a beginning of a *rapprochement* for them. It made a perfect dramatic ending for Emma to decide to reinvent herself as a 'modern woman' and to use that as a re-engagement with Thomas.

As we know, Emma lived another seventeen years after the events depicted in my play. We know that she became more and more isolated and retreated to her rooms in the attic at Max Gate. After she died, apparently without her husband at her side as he was too busy downstairs to attend her despite the maid's calls, Thomas was filled with remorse and went on to write a considerable body of poems in her memory. He soon recovered his composure, however, and married his secretary Florence Dugdale with whom he lived until his death in 1928. Emma's name slipped from the record and much of the written evidence of her life was destroyed in the great burning that Florence carried out after Thomas's death.

And yet. And yet, I still maintain there was some happiness left for Emma. Thomas and Emma managed some sort of public and private life together, bicycling along the dusty byways of Dorset and picnicking at the roadside (Emma sitting in the middle of the road as she didn't care for the insects in the fields). They both had busy, active social lives. Emma gardened and invited in children from the neighbourhood, letting them play among her rose bushes, and occasionally taking them on day trips to Poole or Bournemouth. It was not the life she would have wished for, but it would seem that, for her, the whole of life was a disappointment.

Having lived with Emma for so long now in the writing of this play I have grown fond of her and I see most of her failings as understandable and her eccentricities as endearing foibles. I hope one day there will be a full account of her life; meanwhile, I trust that I have not done her too much of a disservice and have drawn attention to this strange, disappointed woman.

Places to Visit

Max Gate and Hardy's Cottage

Hardy travelled a great deal and there are houses in London, Sturminster Newton and Swanage associated with various parts of his life. However, his birthplace at Higher Bockhampton and Max Gate in Dorchester are essential places to visit. Both are part of the National Trust's 'Hardy Country' group of properties, along with Clouds Hill, the home of Hardy's friend T.E. Lawrence (Lawrence of Arabia) near Wool. The National Trust is putting a great deal of effort into making these properties more able to tell the story of the Great Man. Up to now there has been little to see at Max Gate apart from the bricks and mortar, but new displays are being put in place, the gardens are being restored to their original form and there are events and hands-on experiences throughout the year.

A visit to Max Gate will bring home the type of life that Thomas and Emma enjoyed. You can see how self-sufficient they tried to be, how frugally they lived and how they gardened without harming wildlife to the extent that Thomas would not allow tree branches to be cut when they obscured the light. It is very easy to picture Emma haunting the stair or at work in the garden, while Thomas himself can be envisaged in one of his studies or just disappearing out of the gate in the garden wall when uninvited guests are at the front door.

At the Hardy birthplace in Higher Bockhampton the past has been well preserved and one easily senses what Hardy's early life must have been like. The cottage backs directly onto the heath and is still only accessible via a narrow lane. This is Jemima's domain and visitors can still experience the cooking that went on in the tiny kitchen when Thomas visited his mother on a Sunday afternoon. It is quite possible to walk between the two houses across the water meadows and consider the two women who vied for his attention at either end of the footpath.

Max Gate, Alington Road, Dorchester, DT1 2AB, tel. 01297 489481. OS Grid Ref 194:SY704899

Hardy's Cottage, Higher Bockhampton, Near Dorchester, DT2 8QJ, tel. 01305 262366. OS Grid Ref 194:SY728925.

Dorset County Museum

Among the wealth of galleries in the County Museum and the displays and exhibitions of fossils, roman pavements and Victorian ephemera is the Writer's Dorset collection. The latter explores the lives and work of Dorset's authors, poets and novelists, as well as providing a home to the Ooser – a strange beast (half-man, half-bull) which guards a room full of Dorset music and folk-drama.

A Writer's Dorset celebrates Hardy's achievement and tells the story of his life and work. It uncovers the landscape of his mind, which became the part-real, part-imaginary Wessex of his books – their settings inseparable from the places that inspired them. Perhaps the most significant exhibit is a reconstruction of Hardy's third study from his home at Max Gate. All the furniture, books and personal possessions in the room originally belonged to Hardy. On the desk under the window can be seen the pens that he used to write *Tess of the D'Urbervilles* and *Jude the Obscure*, and a perpetual calendar set at the date of his first meeting with his first wife, Emma Gifford.

Dorset County Museum, High West Street, Dorchester, DT1 1XA, tel. 01305 262735

The Hardy Trail

There are numerous trips that can be taken around Dorset by car, bicycle or foot following the footsteps of Thomas Hardy. They mostly go by the name of the Hardy Trail or something similar. Some concentrate on places he lived and some attempt to match real places with the fictional sites in his books. I did a great deal of this sort of travelling when writing the adaptations of the novels. Some of the sites can be a little prosaic, even disappointing – because, after all, Hardy was creating fiction not a travelogue – but some are absolutely breathtaking and, even if you are not a great Hardy fan, it's a delight to experience the beauty of the Dorset countryside, stopping occasionally for a cream tea or a glass of cider.

Egdon Heath

For me, the quintessential Hardy landscape is that of the open heathland that he called Egdon, the setting for *The Return of the Native*. In reality this is Wareham Forest, sadly mostly now blanketed in Forestry Commission pines and army tank training ranges. Ironically, because the ranges are largely no-go areas, this has preserved large areas of the old heath. You can see this best from the viewpoint at the top of Whiteways Hill where you can enjoy the whole sweep of landscape between the English Channel and Poole Harbour with the preserved heathland of the tank ranges laid out below. You will also see that the Dorset heath was always been a working, managed landscape, with large areas devoted to clay mining and the occasional blackened patch from controlled burning.

If you want to experience what it feels like to walk the heath then possibly the best place is slightly away from Hardy's Egdon at Stoborough Heath between Wareham and Corfe Castle. Take the back road from Stoborough heading for Arne. If you can find a place to park you will soon find yourself lost in this antique landscape. For me, the best time to visit is an early summer dusky evening when the sound of nightjars fills the air. Read the first chapter of *The Return of the Native* before you set out and you will become instantly immersed.

The Dorset History Centre

Finally, something for those with a more specialist interest is the Dorset History Centre. One of the delights of undertaking any literary project is the prospect of doing a bit of historical research. In Dorset we have a fine facility at the Dorset History Centre in Dorchester. Here they keep every sort of record relating to the county (and Bournemouth). So if you are interested in finding out about your family history, the history of your house, the stories of your village or town, or if you want to settle a boundary dispute or even check the history of your car through the licensing records this is a marvellous place to spend the day.

Having signed in at the door with proof of identity you are issued with a ticket that enables you to use all the collections. The Thomas Hardy collection is fascinating and, at the moment, not completely catalogued so there is a bit of rummaging to do. I found all sorts of bits and pieces including photographs and copies of pictures that have never been published. The staff were particularly friendly and helpful and, once they knew what I was after, kept producing boxes and files to hunt through. Obviously, the system works best if you send details of your interest in advance so that boxes can be brought up from the store rooms.

The Dorset History Centre, Bridport Road, Dorchester, DT1 1RP, tel. 01305 250550

About the Author

Peter John Cooper is a professional playwright. He has been associated with many companies including Horseshoe in Basingstoke, the Lyceum in Crewe, Chester Gateway and Theatr Clwyd in North Wales. During the 1980s he was the first artistic director of Oxfordshire Theatre Company and went on to found his own company Spyway Projects with designer Annette Sumption. To date, 28 of his plays have been produced by companies throughout the UK. He has also produced the libretti for four choral works and numerous pieces for radio and theatre in education.

Some of his plays are due to be published online by www.lazybeescripts. co.uk. They range from plays for children, through adaptations of the classics, to his own quirky original pieces. All his works delight in word play and poetry.

Peter was born and brought up in rural Wessex. After living for 20 years in Swanage, he recently moved to the bright lights of Bournemouth. His association with Thomas Hardy goes back to school days. 'As soon as I began reading Hardy it felt as if I was reading about people and places I knew. The more I got to know about the author the more I experienced a fellow feeling. I was brought up on farms and as a young man worked in the fields and felt the harshest of weathers that frequent the Wessex downlands. I was delighted to be given the opportunity to adapt *The Mayor of Casterbridge* for the stage and later *The Trumpet Major*. Even though I knew the countryside well, I always made a point of visiting the sites mentioned in Hardy's works in order to experience Hardy's own relationship with place and interpret that into the text of my works.'

To find out more about Peter visit www.spyway.co.uk and for his poetry and short stories go to spyway.blogspot.com.

The Trumpet Major

Peter John Cooper's stage adaptation of Thomas Hardy's famous novel is now published online at www.lazybeescripts.co.uk.

> Anne Garland sits alone embroidering a tapestry which seems to reflect her memories of the days when she was wooed by two brothers – the wayward and impulsive Bob, the miller's son, and his brother, the honest and upright John, the Trumpet Major. Her choice is complicated by the attentions of Festus Derriman, the cowardly nephew of the local squire.
>
> Anne's indecision causes first one and then the other to slip away and return to her only through misunderstanding and chance. Which one should she choose? And which one did she end up marrying?

Set against the dramatic events of the threatened invasion by the French in the Napoleonic Wars, the play preserves Hardy's sense of place in rural Dorset and also his belief in the greater forces that act upon his protagonists.

Peter's adaptation was originally intended for a small company with minimal setting but there is plenty of scope for productions with larger casts and sets. It is both funny and melancholy, with the set pieces of the night of Napoleon's invasion in stark contrast to the wryly gentle love scenes. The play was originally commissioned by the Oxfordshire Theatre Company where Peter was first Artistic Director.

'Skilfully adapted dialogue'

– *The Oxford Times*

Lazybee will deal with all performance issues including rights and charges for *The Trumpet Major* and for others of Peter John Cooper's works for theatre. Look out for further Hardy adaptations and original plays at Lazybee.

The Thomas Hardy Society

At our biennial International Conference in July 2010, *She Opened the Door*, as the last item on the programme, successfully closed the event, with 'house full' notices at the Dorchester Corn Exchange. This is what the Hardy Society does: promoting Hardy to both students and general readers alike, encouraging people to explore the extraordinary world Hardy portrayed in his novels and poetry – world famous novels like *Far From the Madding Crowd* and *Tess of the d'Urbervilles*, coupled with arguably some of the greatest love poetry ever published in English. Coach tours and walks bring to life the still-recognisable countryside Hardy wrote about nearly 150 years ago, and the musical heritage, often never far beneath the surface of his work, is part of the programme.

To find out more about what the Society does please go to
www.hardysociety.org or email info@hardysociety.org.

Mike Nixon
Secretary,
Thomas Hardy Society

About Roving Press

We are a small Dorset-based publisher producing local-interest books for those who like to get out and explore. We publish only a handful of new titles each year which we enjoy and believe in, working very closely with authors to produce high-quality books that are practical and affordable for readers. New writers are welcome to contact us.

Our website (**www.rovingpress.co.uk**) gives information about us, our books and our authors. Author-signed copies are available on request. Drop us your details and we'll let you know as other local titles become available that might be of interest.

Other Roving Press Titles

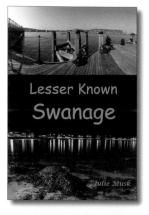

Lesser Known **Swanage**

Julie Musk

The **SPIRIT OF PORTLAND**
Revelations of a Sacred Isle

Gary Biltcliffe

Roaring Dorset!
Encounters with Big Cats

Merrily Harpur

THE PORTLAND CHRONICLES

THE PORTLAND SEA DRAGON

CAROL HUNT

THE PORTLAND CHRONICLES

ENCHANTMENT OF THE BLACK DOG

CAROL HUNT

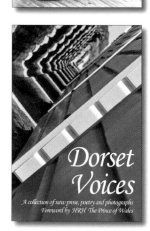

THE PORTLAND CHRONICLES

PORTLAND PIRATES

CAROL HUNT

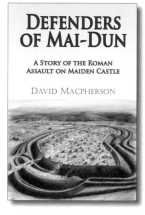

DEFENDERS OF MAI-DUN

A STORY OF THE ROMAN ASSAULT ON MAIDEN CASTLE

DAVID MACPHERSON

Kids' Dorset

Roving Press

Dorset Voices

A collection of new prose, poetry and photographs
Foreword by HRH The Prince of Wales

If you like exploring, you'll love our books